RUNNING ON EMPTY

Jonice Webb has written a terrific book about what you didn't get in childhood - what wasn't there that should have been: guidance, attunement; in some cases, love. The damage caused by emotional neglect and what to do to heal it are the subjects of this exciting, readable, and potentially life changing work.

—**Terrence Real**
Internationally Recognized Family Therapist & Bestselling Author
Regular Contributor on Good Morning America & ABC News

In a compelling and articulate way, *Running on Empty* shines an important light on the emotional legacy passed down to us from our parents. It helps make clear how the parenting we receive as children affects us emotionally and socially in adulthood. In a rich, warm, empathic voice, Dr. Webb speaks directly to us, helping us identify our emotional roadblocks, and providing a path through them.

—**Jeffrey Pickar, Ph.D.**
Clinical Instructor in Psychology
Department of Psychiatry
Harvard Medical School

Reading Dr. Webb's *Running on Empty* immediately impacted my work as a child and adolescent psychologist. Her conceptualization of emotional neglect and its myriad effects on the developing child is crystal clear, and one that I have not seen elsewhere. Dr. Webb provides tools so clinicians can identify patterns of emotional neglect that may be occurring in the families with whom they are working. More importantly, *Running on Empty* offers the clinician practical guidelines to help parents of children and adolescents stop emotional neglect in its tracks.

Stephanie M. Kriesberg, Psy.D.
Child and Adolescent Psychologist
Lexington, MA

RUNNINGON EMPTY

*Overcome Your Childhood
Emotional Neglect*

Jonice Webb, PhD
with **Christine Musello, PsyD**

NEW YORK

RUNNING ON EMPTY

Overcome Your Childhood Emotional Neglect

Published in New York, New York, by Morgan James Publishing. Morgan James is a trademark of Morgan James, LLC. www.MorganJamesPublishing.com

ISBN 978-1-61448-242-0 paperback
ISBN 978-1-63047-104-0 hard cover
ISBN 978-1-61448-243-7 eBook
Library of Congress Control Number: 2012931742

Cover Design by:
Rachel Lopez
www.r2cdesign.com

Morgan James is a proud partner of Habitat for Humanity Peninsula
and Greater Williamsburg. Partners in building since 2006.

Get involved today! Visit
www.MorganJamesBuilds.com

Dedicated to My Clients

TABLE OF CONTENTS

PREFACE

Writing this book has been one of the most fascinating experiences of my life. As the concept of Emotional Neglect gradually became clearer and more defined in my head, it changed not only the way I practiced psychology, but also the way I looked at the world. I started to see Emotional Neglect everywhere: in the way I sometimes parented my own children or treated my husband, at the mall, and even on reality TV shows. I found myself often thinking that it would help people enormously if they could become aware of this invisible force that affects us all: Emotional Neglect.

After watching the concept become a vital aspect of my work over several years, and becoming fully convinced of its value, I finally shared it with my colleague, Dr. Christine Musello. Christine responded with immediate understanding, and quickly began seeing Emotional Neglect in her own clinical practice, and all around her, as I had. Together we started to work on outlining and defining the phenomenon. Dr. Musello was helpful in the process of putting the initial words to the concept of Emotional Neglect. The fact that she was so readily able to embrace the concept, and found it so useful, encouraged me to take it forward.

Although Dr. Musello was not able to continue in the writing of this book with me, she was a helpful support at the beginning of the writing process. She composed some of the first sections of the book and several of the clinical vignettes. I am therefore pleased to recognize her contribution.

ACKNOWLEDGMENTS

This book never could have been imagined or written without the willingness of the clients featured in the vignettes to share their stories and pain in therapy. It is with great appreciation and respect that I express my deepest thanks for their trust, candor and commitment.

Also, many thanks to *The New Yorker* for working with me so that I could use some of their excellent cartoons to add humor and spice to *Running on Empty*.

To write this book, I have needed to rely on the tremendous knowledge and support of my family, friends and colleagues. I would like to thank a few of the many people who have kept me going, and helped me throughout this process.

First, I would like to express my deepest gratitude to Denise Waldron, who took countless hours away from writing her own book to read and edit this manuscript. Denise's eye for detail was invaluable. She continually amazed me by catching the large and small inconsistencies and errors, and helping me to set them right.

Second, I wish to thank Joanie Schaffner, LICSW, Dr. Danielle DeTora, and Nicholas Brown for their excellent feedback and ideas for how to make the manuscript better; Michael Feinstein for offering his business savvy at times when I was making complicated and difficult decisions; and my agent, Michael Ebeling, for believing in my book and in me, and for guiding me through the complicated publishing process.

Dr. Scott Creighton, Catherine Bergh, Patrice and Chuck Abernathy, David Hornstein and Nancy Fitzgerald Heckman each offered a special boost when I needed it, by listening, caring, advising, or asking favors of others to help make this book happen.

Lastly, I want to express my heartfelt love and appreciation to my husband, Seth Davis and my two children, Lydia and Isaac, for willingly weathering my long hours of researching and writing, and for never letting me doubt myself. There is no way I could have written this book without their support and unwavering confidence sustaining me.

INTRODUCTION

What do you remember from your childhood? Almost everyone remembers some bits and pieces, if not more. Perhaps you have some positive memories, like family vacations, teachers, friends, summer camps or academic awards; and some negative memories, like family conflicts, sibling rivalries, problems at school, or even some sad or troubling events. *Running on Empty* is not about any of those kinds of memories. In fact, it's not about anything that you can remember or anything that happened in your childhood. This book is written to help you become aware of what *didn't happen* in your childhood, what you *don't remember.* Because *what didn't happen* has as much or more power over who you have become as an adult than any of those events you do remember. *Running on Empty* will introduce you to the consequences of what didn't happen: an invisible force that may be at work in your life. I will help you determine whether you've been affected by this invisible force and, if so, how to overcome it.

Many fine, high-functioning, capable people secretly feel unfulfilled or disconnected. "Shouldn't I be happier?" "Why haven't I accomplished more?" "Why doesn't my life feel more meaningful?" These are questions which are often prompted by the invisible force at work. They are often asked by people who believe that they had loving, well-meaning parents, and who remember their childhood as mostly happy and healthy. So they blame themselves for whatever doesn't feel right as an adult. They don't realize that they are under the influence of what they don't remember ... the invisible force.

By now, you're probably wondering, *what is this Invisible Force?* Rest assured it's nothing scary. It's not supernatural, psychic or eerie. It's actually a very common, human thing that *doesn't happen* in homes and families all over the world every day. Yet we don't realize it exists, matters or has any impact upon us at all. We don't have a word for it. We don't think about it and we don't talk about it. We can't see it; we can only feel it. And when we do feel it, we don't know what we're feeling.

In this book, I'm finally giving this force a name. I'm calling it Emotional Neglect. This is not to be confused with physical neglect. Let's talk about what Emotional Neglect really is.

Everyone is familiar with the word "neglect." It's a common word. The definition of "neglect," according to the Merriam-Webster Dictionary, is "to give little attention or respect or to disregard; to leave unattended to, especially through carelessness."

"Neglect" is a word used especially frequently by mental health professionals in the Social Services. It's commonly used to refer to a dependent person, such as a child or elder, whose *physical* needs are not being met. For example a child who comes to school with no coat in the winter, or an elder shut-in whose adult daughter frequently "forgets" to bring her groceries.

Pure *emotional* neglect is invisible. It can be extremely subtle, and it rarely has any physical or visible signs. In fact, many *emotionally* neglected children have received excellent physical care. Many come from families that seem ideal. The people for whom I write this book are unlikely to have been identified as neglected by any outward signs, and are in fact unlikely to have been identified as neglected at all.

So why write a book? After all, if the topic of Emotional Neglect has gone unnoticed by researchers and professionals all this time, how debilitating can it really be? The truth is, people suffering from Emotional Neglect are in pain. But they can't figure out why, and too often, neither can the therapists treating them. In writing this book, I identify, define and suggest solutions to a hidden struggle that often stymies its sufferers and even the professionals to whom they sometimes go for help. My goal is to help these people who are suffering in silence, wondering what is wrong with them.

There is a good explanation for why Emotional Neglect has been so overlooked. *It hides.* It dwells in the sins of omission, rather than commission; it's the white space in the family picture rather than the picture itself. It's often what was NOT said or observed or remembered from childhood, rather than what WAS said.

For example, parents may provide a lovely home and plenty of food and clothing, and never abuse or mistreat their child. But these same parents may fail to notice their teen child's drug use or simply give him too much freedom rather than set the limits that would lead to conflict. When that teen is an adult, he may look back at an "ideal" childhood, never realizing that his parents failed him in the way that he needed them most. He may blame himself for whatever difficulties have ensued from his poor choices as a teen. "I was a real handful"; "I had such a great childhood, I have no excuse for not having achieved more in life." As a therapist, I have heard these words uttered many times by high-functioning, wonderful people who are unaware that Emotional Neglect

"This song is dedicated to our parents, and is in the form of a plea for more adequate supervision."

XVIII | RUNNING ON EMPTY

was an invisible, powerful force in their childhood. This example offers only one of the infinite numbers of ways that a parent can emotionally neglect a child, leaving him running on empty.

Here I would like to insert a very important caveat: We *all* have examples of how our parents have failed us here and there. No parent is perfect, and no childhood is perfect. We know that the huge majority of parents struggle to do what's best for their child. Those of us who are parents know that when we make parenting mistakes, we can almost always correct them. This book is not meant to shame parents or make parents feel like failures. In fact, throughout the book you'll read about many parents who are loving and well-meaning, but still emotionally neglected their child in some fundamental way. Many emotionally neglectful parents are fine people and good parents, but were emotionally neglected themselves as children. *All* parents commit occasional acts of Emotional Neglect in raising their children without causing any real harm. It only becomes a problem when it is of a great enough breadth or quantity to gradually emotionally "starve" the child.

Whatever the level of parental failure, emotionally neglected people see themselves as the problem, rather than seeing their parents as having failed them.

Throughout the book I include many examples, or vignettes, taken from the lives of my clients and others, those who have grappled with sadness or anxiety or emptiness in their lives, for which there were no words and for which they could find little explanation. These emotionally neglected people most often know how to give others what they want or need. They know what is expected from them in most of life's social environments. Yet these sufferers are unable to label and describe what is wrong in their internal experience of life and how it harms them.

This is not to say that adults who were emotionally neglected as children are without observable symptoms. But these symptoms, the ones that may have brought them to a psychotherapist's door, always masquerade as something else: depression, marital problems, anxiety, anger. Adults who have been emotionally neglected mislabel their unhappiness in such ways, and tend to feel embarrassed by asking for help. Since they have not learned to identify or to be in touch with their true emotional needs, it's difficult for therapists to keep them in treatment long enough to help them understand themselves better. So this book is written not only for the emotionally neglected, but also for mental health professionals, who need tools to combat the chronic lack of compassion-for-self which can sabotage the best of treatments.

Whether you picked up *Running on Empty* because you are looking for answers to your own feelings of emptiness and lack of fulfillment, or because you are a mental health professional trying to help "stuck" patients, this book will provide concrete solutions for invisible wounds.

In *Running on Empty*, I have used many vignettes to illustrate various aspects of Emotional Neglect in childhood and adulthood. All of the vignettes are based upon real stories from clinical practice, either my own or Dr. Musello's. However, to protect the privacy of the clients, names, identifying facts, and details were altered, so that no vignette depicts any real person, living or dead. The exceptions are the vignettes involving Zeke which appear throughout Chapters 1 and 2. These vignettes were created to illustrate how different parenting styles might affect the same boy, and are purely fictitious.

Emotional Neglect Questionnaire

When Emotional Neglect happens to a child, it is often subtle, invisible and unmemorable. As an adult you may be wondering, "Then how can I know if I have it?"

This dilemma is the exact reason I created the Emotional Neglect Questionnaire (The ENQ). It's a series of questions for you to answer Yes or No. Your score will not only give you an idea about whether you have CEN; it will also give you a window into the areas in which your CEN occurred.

To take the ENQ, go to:

www.drjonicewebb.com/cen-questionnaire

Click on the **Take the Questionnaire** button. Enter your email, and the ENQ will be sent to you at that same address.

PART I

RUNNING ON EMPTY

Chapter 1

WHY WASN'T
THE TANK FILLED?

"...I am trying to draw attention to the immense contribution to the individual and to society which the ordinary good mother with her husband in support makes at the beginning, and which she does *simply through being devoted to her infant.*"

D.W. Winnicott, (1964) *The Child, the Family, and the Outside World*

I t doesn't take a parenting guru, a saint, or, thank goodness, a Ph.D. in psychology to raise a child to be a healthy, happy adult. The child psychiatrist, researcher, writer and psychoanalyst Donald Winnicott emphasized this point often throughout writings that spanned 40 years. While today we recognize that fathers are of equal importance in the development of a child, the meaning of Winnicott's observations on mothering is still essentially the same: There is a *minimal* amount of parental emotional connection, empathy and ongoing attention which is necessary to fuel a child's growth and development so that he or she will grow into an emotionally healthy and emotionally connected adult. Less than that minimal amount and the child becomes an adult who

3

struggles emotionally–outwardly successful, perhaps, but empty, missing something within, which the world can't see.

In his writings, Winnicott coined the now well-known term, "Good Enough Mother" to describe a mother who meets her child's needs in this way. Parenting that is "good enough" takes many forms, but all of these recognize the child's emotional or physical need in any given moment, in any given culture, and do a "good enough" job of meeting it. Most parents are good enough. Like all animals, we humans are biologically wired to raise our children to thrive. But what happens when life circumstances interfere with parenting? Or when parents themselves are unhealthy, or have significant character flaws?

Were you raised by "good enough" parents? By the end of this chapter, you will know what "good enough" means, and you will be able to answer this question for yourself.

But first...

If you are a parent as well as a reader, you may find yourself identifying with the parental *failures* presented in this book, as well as with the emotional experience of the child in the vignettes (because you are, no doubt, hard on yourself.) Therefore, I ask that you pay close attention to the following warnings:

First

All good parents are guilty of emotionally failing their children at times. Nobody is perfect. We all get tired, cranky, stressed, distracted, bored, confused, disconnected, overwhelmed or otherwise compromised here and there. This does not qualify us as emotionally neglectful parents. Emotionally neglectful parents distinguish themselves in one of two ways, and often both: either they emotionally fail their child in some critical way in a moment of crisis, causing the child a wound which may never be repaired (acute empathic failure) OR they are chronically tone-deaf to some aspect of a child's need throughout his or her childhood development (chronic empathic failure). Every single parent on earth can recall a parenting failure that makes him cringe, where he knows that he has failed his child. But the harm comes from the totality of important moments in which emotionally neglectful parents are deaf and blind to the <u>emotional</u> needs of their growing child.

Second

If you were indeed emotionally neglected, and are a parent yourself as well, there is a good chance that as you read this book you will start to see some ways in which you have passed the torch of Emotional Neglect to your child. If so, it's extremely vital for you to realize that *it is not your fault*. Because it's invisible, insidious, and easily passes from generation to generation, it's extremely unlikely and difficult to stop unless you become explicitly aware of it. Since you're reading this book, you are light-years ahead of your parents. You have the opportunity to change the pattern, and you are taking it. The effects of Emotional Neglect can be reversed. And you're about to learn how to reverse those parental patterns for yourself, and for your children. Keep reading. *No self-blame allowed.*

The Ordinary Healthy Parent in Action

The importance of emotion in healthy parenting is best understood through attachment theory. Attachment theory describes how our emotional needs for safety and connection are met by our parents from infancy. Many ways of looking at human behavior have grown out of attachment theory, but most owe their thinking to the original attachment theorist, psychiatrist John Bowlby. His understanding of parent-child bonding comes from thousands of hours of observation of parents and children, beginning with mothers and infants. It suggests, quite simply, that when a parent effectively recognizes and meets her child's emotional needs in infancy, a "secure attachment" is formed and maintained. This first attachment forms the basis of a positive self-image and a sense of general well-being throughout childhood and into adulthood.

Looking at emotional health through the lens of attachment theory, we can identify three essential emotional skills in parents:

1) The parent **feels an emotional connection** to the child.
2) The parent **pays attention** to the child and sees him as a unique and separate person, rather than, say, an extension of him or herself, a possession or a burden.
3) Using that **emotional connection** and **paying attention**, the parent **responds competently** to the child's **emotional need**.

Although these skills sound simple, in combination they are a powerful tool for helping a child learn about and manage his or her own nature, for creating a secure emotional bond that carries the child into adulthood, so that he may face the world with the emotional health to achieve a happy adulthood. In short, when parents are mindful of their children's unique emotional nature, they raise emotionally strong adults. Some parents are able to do this intuitively, but others can learn the skills. Either way, the child will not be neglected.

ZEKE

Zeke is a precocious and hyperactive third-grader, the youngest of 3 children in a laid-back and loving family. Lately, he has gotten into trouble at school for "talking back." On one such day, he brings a note home from the teacher describing his infraction by stating "Zeke was disrespectful today." His mother sits him down and asks him what happened. In an exasperated tone, he tells her that, when he was in the recess line, Mrs. Rollo told him to stop trying to balance a pencil on his finger, point-side-up, because he might "stab himself in the face." He frowned and snapped back at Mrs. Rollo by telling her that he would have to bend "alllll the way over the pencil like this" (demonstrating) to stab himself in the face and that he isn't "that stupid." In response, Mrs. Rollo confiscated his pencil, wrote his name on the board, and sent him home with a note.

Before describing how Zeke's mother actually responded, let's figure out what Zeke needs to get from the coming parent-child interaction: he is upset by the incident with his teacher, whom he generally likes, so he needs empathy; on the other hand, he also needs to learn what is expected of him by his teachers in order to succeed at school. Finally, it would help if his mother has noticed (emotional attentiveness) that lately he is very sensitive to "being treated like a baby" because his older brother and sister leave him out a lot due to his age. Zeke's mother needs those three skills: feeling a connection, paying attention, and responding competently, in order to help Zeke with his problem.

Here is how the conversation went between mother and son:

Mother: "Mrs. Rollo didn't understand that you were <u>embarrassed</u> by her thinking you could be stupid enough to stick your eye out with a pencil. But when teachers ask you to stop doing something, the reason doesn't matter. It's your job to stop."

Zeke: "I know! I was trying to say that to her and she wouldn't listen!"

Mother: "Yes, I know how <u>frustrated</u> you get when people don't let you talk. Mrs. Rollo doesn't know that you're dealing with your brother and sister not listening to you much lately."

Zeke relaxes a little in response to his mother's understanding: "Yeah, she got me so <u>frustrated</u> and then she took my pencil."

*Mother: "It must've been hard for you. But, you see, Mrs. Rollo's class is very big and she doesn't have time to talk things over like we are right now. It's **so** important that <u>when any grownup at school asks you to do something, you do it right</u>*

> *away. Will you try to do as asked without saying anything back, Zeke?"*
>
> *Zeke: "Yeah, Mom."*
>
> *Mother: "Good! <u>If you do what Mrs. Rollo asks, you'll never get in trouble.</u> Then you can come home and complain to us if you think it's unfair. That's fine. But as a student, respect means cooperating with your teacher's requests."*

This mother's intuitive responses in the above conversation provide us with a complex example of the healthy, emotionally attuned parenting that leads to the sane, happy adult whom Winnicott describes. What exactly did she do?

- First, she connected with her son emotionally by asking him to tell her what happened *before* she reacted. No shaming.
- Then she listened carefully to him. When she first spoke, she provided him with a simple rule that an eight-year-old can understand: "When a teacher asks you to do something, you do it right away." Here Zeke's mother is instinctively attuned to his stage of cognitive development, providing him with a general rule to use at school.
- She immediately follows the rule with empathy and *naming* his feeling *("Mrs. Rollo didn't understand that you were **embarrassed**...").* Hearing his mom name the feeling, Zeke is able to express more of his emotion to his mother *("I know! I was trying to say that to her and she wouldn't listen!").*
- Again, his mother responds to Zeke by naming or labeling the emotion that drove Zeke's rude behavior towards his teacher, the behavior of contradicting her that was viewed as disrespectful *("Yes. I know how **frustrated** you get when people don't let you talk...").*
- Zeke, feeling understood, responds by repeating this emotion word for himself, *"Yeah, she got me so **frustrated** and then she took my pencil."*

- But the mother isn't finished yet. She has, in this conversation, demonstrated to Zeke that she understands him and feels for him by demonstrating that she sees his behavior differently than his teacher does. However, she can't stop there, because his tendency to debate (the likely result of having two highly verbal older siblings) *will continue* to be a problem for Zeke at school unless he can correct it. So his mom says "*It's so important that when any grownup at school asks you to do something, you do it right away.*"
- Finally, she holds her son accountable for his behavior, setting the stage for future check-ins on his feisty nature by asking him, "Will you try to do as asked without saying anything back, Zeke?"

In a conversation that appears deceptively simple, Zeke's mother has avoided shaming him for a mistake and named his feelings, creating the emotional learning that will allow Zeke to sort his feelings out on his own in the future. She has also supported him emotionally, given him a social rule, and asked him to be accountable for following it. And, in the event that Zeke repeats this behavior at school, she will adjust her message and her actions to adapt to the difficulty he is having in the classroom.

Remember Zeke, because I will be using him several more times to help describe the differences between healthy and emotionally neglectful parenting.

Here's another example:

KATHLEEN

Frequently, harmful Emotional Neglect is so subtle in the life of a child that, although it may be in play each and every day, it's barely observable, often masking as a form of consideration or even indulgence.

Kathleen is a successful, recently married young woman who makes a great salary as an executive assistant in a small high-tech, start-up company. She persuaded her new husband to buy a home with her in the town in which her parents live. Yet she did so knowing that, as she revealed in therapy, her mother often drove her crazy. She was puzzled by her own decision-making. She recognized that her mother had always demanded a lot of her attention, and was aware that she felt guilty about her mother, no matter how much attention she gave her. At the time she came to therapy, at the height of her success and happiness: new home, new husband, great job, Kathleen felt inexplicably depressed. She was both ashamed of and baffled by this feeling, since there was "no reason for it." What follows is a good example of how Emotional Neglect hides, not in what did happen, but in what *didn't happen.*

> *Flash back twenty-five years and five-year-old Kathleen is sitting on the beach, happily making sandcastles with her father. The only child of a successful young couple, living in a pristine restored New England home, people often tell her how lucky she is. Dad is an engineer, and Mom has gone back to school and become an elementary school teacher. Travel to exotic places and being taught meticulous manners are part of Kathleen's life. Kathleen's mom, an excellent seamstress, makes her clothes. Often they wear mother/daughter matching outfits. They spend tons of time together. But right now, on vacation, she has left the matching beach chair at her mother's side. Why? Because her dad has just invited her to play. She has the rare and pleasurable opportunity to be doing something special with her dad. They are digging a hole, collecting the sand to form the first floor of their sand castles.*
>
> *Mom looks up from her book after a while, and, from the perch of her beach chair, says sternly, "That's enough sandplay with Dad, Kathleen. Your Dad doesn't want to have to play with you all day on his day off! Come over here and I'll read to you." Both Dad and daughter look up from their hole, plastic shovels poised. There is a brief pause. Then her father stands up and brushes the sand off his knees as if he, too, must obey.*

Kathleen feels sad as the play stops, but she also feels selfish. Mom takes good care of both of them, and Kathleen shouldn't wear her dad out. She goes obediently over to her smaller, matching beach chair, and sits in it. Her mother begins to read to her. After a while, Kathleen's disappointment passes as she listens to the story.

In our therapy, Kathleen relayed this memory in the course of explaining how distant a relationship she had always had with her father. But when she got to the part where her father stood up and brushed the sand from his knees, her eyes welled up with tears. "I don't know why that image makes me so sad," she said. I asked her to focus on her sadness and think about what else her mother or father might have done differently that day. At that moment, Kathleen began to see that she had been failed frequently by *both* parents. It wasn't hard to figure out what she would have wanted to be different that day. She just wished that she could have continued digging that hole with her father.

If her mother had been emotionally-attuned to Kathleen:

Mom looks up from her book as they play, and from the perch of her beach chair says with a smile, "Wow, you guys are certainly digging a big hole! Want me to show you how to make a sandcastle?"

Or

If her father had been emotionally-attuned:

Mom looks up from her book as they play, and, from the perch of her beach chair says sternly, "That's enough sandplay with Dad, Kathleen. Your dad doesn't want to have to play with you all day on his day off! Come over here and I'll read to you." Both Dad and daughter look up. There is a brief pause. Dad smiles broadly, first at his wife and then at Kathleen. "Are you kidding? There is

no place else I'd rather be than playing with my girl on the beach!
Want to help us dig, Margaret?"

What's important to notice about both of these "corrections" is that they are well within the range of ordinary, natural parenting skills. Conversations like these go on all the time. But if there is an absence of such validation of a child's importance to the parent, if a child is made to feel shame for wanting or needing attention from one parent or the other often enough, *she will grow up being blind to many of her own emotional needs.* Happily, the adult Kathleen came to recognize that there was a good reason for her anger at her mother. She saw that hiding behind the scenes in their mother/daughter relationship all these years had been her mother's lack of emotional attunement to her. Once Kathleen recognized that her anger was legitimate, she felt less guilty for having it. She realized that it was okay to stop catering to her mother and do what was right for her and her husband. Also, a door was opened for Kathleen to understand her mother's limitations, and to try to repair their relationship.

Another important factor in the Kathleen scenario is that Kathleen's parents haven't committed any great parenting offense. Their "mistake" is so subtle that neither was probably the tiniest bit aware that anything damaging was happening for their daughter. In fact, they were probably just living out the patterns that were passed on to them in their own childhoods. This is the danger of Emotional Neglect: perfectly good people, loving their child, doing their best, while passing on accidental, invisible, potentially damaging patterns to their daughter. In this book, the goal is not to blame the parents. It is only to understand our parents, and how they have affected us.

Now that you have a sense of the difference between healthy and neglectful parenting, let's move on to look at the specific types of neglectful parents. As you read this section, see if you can recognize your own parents among them.

Chapter 2

TWELVE WAYS TO END UP EMPTY

T here are an infinite number of ways for a parent to fail a child emotionally. There are so many that it would be impossible to cover them all in this book. What we can do is take a look at the most pertinent categories of parents. Please read this with an understanding that your particular parents may have traits from one type combined with traits of another. Even if you think you have your parents pegged after reading the first type, it may be helpful to read all the way to the end of the chapter. It's entirely possible that you'll see something in Type 9 that you've experienced yourself after having already identified your parents as Type 5, for example. All of these examples are meant to be "mix-and-match," although the majority of parents fit predominantly into one identifiable type.

I've saved the largest category for the end: the Well-Meaning-But-Neglected-Themselves parents. This category talks about the many, many parents who fail their child emotionally, but who have all the best of intentions. They have their children's best interests in mind. They love their children genuinely and truly. They just don't know how to give their children what they need. If you read Type 1 through Type 11 and none of them seem right, it's very possible that you were raised by WMBNT parents.

Type 1: The Narcissistic Parent

Perhaps you are familiar with the Greek myth of Narcissus, from which the word "narcissistic" is derived. In the myth, Narcissus was a strikingly handsome young man whose looks dazzled all who knew him. Many praised him and fell in love with him, but he was so vain that he rejected them all. No one was good enough for him! Eventually, Narcissus saw and fell in love with his reflection in a pool of water. Unable to walk away from his own image, he either committed suicide or wasted away, depending on the version of the myth.

Narcissistic people are a lot like their namesake. Most of the time, they run on a full tank of superiority, confidence and charisma. But sometimes narcissists recognize that their sense of superiority to others is an illusion. Therefore, they gravitate towards evidence that confirms that sense of superiority, and they avoid interactions or relationships that provide evidence to the contrary. When someone or something shatters their grandiose sense of themselves, they become difficult. Despite their arrogance, they're easily hurt and emotionally weak. They hold grudges, blame failures on others, banish people to the doghouse, and tantrum when things don't go their way. They don't like to be wrong. They like to hear themselves talk. But perhaps their most damaging trait is that they often judge others and find them sadly lacking. They are the Kings and Queens of any family, office or enterprise.

You can imagine that when narcissists become parents, they demand perfection from their children or at the very least, no embarrassment. While healthy parents may cringe a little when their child fails to catch the fly ball in the big game, the narcissist parent of that child is angry and feels personally humiliated. When their children make mistakes that are visible to others—no matter how much they may need their parents' help at that time—narcissists take it personally and make their children pay.

SID

Nineteen-year-old Sid is standing at the front door of his wealthy parents' well-appointed home. He is a tall, handsome young man at first glance. But look into his eyes and you see pain and uncertainty. His hands are clasped in front of him and his shoulders slightly hunched. A policeman stands beside him and rings the doorbell. The policeman and the young man wait for several minutes until an elegant woman opens the door. She gives the policeman a charming smile and thanks him for bringing her son home, takes the paperwork that he hands her, and steps aside to let her son enter. The policeman leaves. Sid's mother closes the front door and for a moment stands in front of her son, with arms folded, a firm, impenetrable look on her face. Sid leans slightly toward her, as if wanting, or perhaps hoping, for physical contact.

She says, "Your father is very upset. You can't talk to him now. He went to bed. Go sleep in your old room and we will discuss this in the morning."

Has Sid been caught drinking? Or has he done something more serious, stealing perhaps?

*No. Sid, who hasn't been driving long, has just hit and critically injured a pedestrian with his car. He has just hit a man who had been dashing across a busy street to catch the bus, a man in his forties with a family. He is now in the hospital in a coma. **And Sid's mother sends him to his room.** She is upset because she knows that tomorrow his name will be in the paper, bringing shame to the family.*

Narcissistic parents don't really recognize their children as people separate from them. Instead, they see their children as little extensions of themselves. The needs of the child are defined by the needs of the parent, and the child who tries to express his needs is often accused of being selfish or inconsiderate.

BEATRICE

Beatrice was a bright fourteen-year-old African American girl who got a full scholarship to a renowned and prestigious private high school in her town. Most of the students were so rich that they travelled to places like Monte Carlo or the Swiss Alps on school breaks. But Beatrice was a "townie" whose parents had to save just to take her to Disney World or Cape Cod once a year. At her new school, her grades were fine, as usual. But she was miserable all year, feeling like the token black, the token townie and most of all like she didn't belong.

*Throughout the school year, however, Beatrice's mother was in heaven. She loved dressing up and going to school events to rub shoulders with Senators and Wall Street parents. She loved talking to her neighbors about how difficult the school was, and how well Beatrice was doing. She felt that she was finally socializing with the type of people that interested her. Whenever Beatrice tried to express her social misery, her mother would exclaim, "This is a wonderful opportunity for you to be super-successful in life! It's only 4 years. You just need to toughen up!" Beatrice tried to take her mother's words to heart, but she was lonely, depressed and had little in common with the other students. When she told her parents at the end of the school year that she was going back to her public school, her mother blew up, burst into tears and shouted, "How could you do this **to me**? Now I won't see all my wonderful friends there! And our neighbors will be so glad you failed because they were jealous of me! You're doing all of this because you are nothing but a selfish drama queen!" Beatrice's dad was no help. He had learned it was best to side with mom.*

What Beatrice needed was compassion and understanding. What she got was shame. For a very long time, her mother had a hard time forgiving her for a choice which, by the way, proved to be the right one for Beatrice. She graduated from public school with a full scholarship to Brown, and her mother was happy again.

What the narcissistic parent lacks is the ability to imagine or care about what her children feel. A parent without empathy is like a surgeon operating with dull tools in poor lighting. The results are likely to produce scarring.

ZEKE

Back to Zeke, the third grader who in Chapter 1 disrespected his teacher and was sent home with a note. Here's the interaction he might have with his mother if she were a narcissist:

Zeke hands his mother the note. She reads it and Zeke sees her muscles tensing, her jaw tightening and a flush stealing up her neck. She shakes the note in Zeke's face: "How could you do this, Zeke? Now Ms. Rollo will think I've not taught you good manners! This is embarrassing. Go to your room. I don't want to see you right now. I'm very hurt."

Zeke's mother took his misbehavior personally, as if he had done it **to her.** She's not concerned about Zeke, his feelings or his behavior. This is all about her. Therefore, he got no useful advice or feedback about how to get along at school.

When narcissists become parents, they are apt to have very different relationships with each of their children. They play favorites and often find at least one of their children a disappointment. But the one child who reflects them well, by being handsome or pretty or athletic or intelligent, is the "anointed one" and enjoys a special relationship with narcissist mommy or daddy. It is sometimes only in adulthood that the favored child of a narcissist realizes that her parent's love has been conditional all along.

GINA

Gina is a 32-year-old woman, the oldest of three children from an old Manhattan family. Up until very recently, she has been the apple of her father's eye and has enjoyed a good, close relationship with him. Yet her younger brother, who has always been less successful than she, keeps his distance from their father, and also from Gina herself. Gina has never understood why that is and chalks it up to her brother being jealous. Now, however, Gina is getting married to a second-generation immigrant man, a successful lawyer at her law firm. He is a man, however, whom her father feels is beneath her. Since their engagement, her father is cold to her and avoids her calls. When they do talk, he uses that critical tone that Gina has always heard being directed at her brother. Gina understands that she is disappointing her father. At age 32, she's finally able to see why her brother has detached himself from the family.

With this new awareness, Gina may go forward in life distancing from her father. But she may always subconsciously try to please him, to be better than the rest and to gather accolades and praise just for him. She is trapped in her father's mirror. Throughout childhood, her own identity was neglected while she toiled to fulfill her father's grandiose ideas of what a perfect daughter she was. Whether the child of the narcissist feels hated growing up, like Gina's brother, or feels loved, as Gina did, in adulthood that long-ago child will struggle to free himself from the narcissist's judgment. He will struggle to see himself through his own eyes.

I'm sure you're starting to get the idea. Emotionally neglectful parenting can look a lot like healthy parenting at first glance. But the differences are dramatic. Just as in the forest one mushroom can be dinner and the other can be deadly, the similarities are on the surface alone. The coming chapters will teach you how to recognize the various poisonous mushrooms, how to become fully alive, and how to pass that strength and knowledge on to the next generation.

Type 2: The Authoritarian Parent

In 1966, the psychologist Dr. Diana Baumrind was the first to identify and describe "The Authoritarian Parent." Dr. Baumrind described authoritarian parents as rule-bound, restrictive and punitive, raising their children based upon very inflexible and unbending demands. The phrases most likely to come to mind when considering authoritarian parents are:

"Old school"

"Children are meant to be seen and not heard"

"Spare the rod, spoil the child"

If you are a Baby Boomer (born between 1946 and 1964) or older, you have a better chance of having been raised by authoritarian parents. This parenting style was more popular among parents of that era. Today's parents tend to adopt a much more open and permissive approach, often fueled by a conscious decision NOT to raise their own children as they themselves were raised. However, there are certainly plenty of authoritarian parents still in existence.

Authoritarian parents require a lot from their children. The children are expected to follow their parents' rules without questioning them. At the same time, these parents don't explain the reasons behind their rules. They simply require adherence, and crack down harshly when the child doesn't comply. Authoritarian parents are more likely to punish or spank rather than they are to discuss a problem or issue with their child. They are not particularly concerned with the feelings or ideas of the child. They parent according to a template they have in their own heads of what a generic child's behavior should be, and do not take into account the individual needs, temperament or feelings of their particular child.

Most abusive parents fall into the authoritarian category. However, Dr. Baumrind is careful to point out that *not all authoritarian parents are abusive.* I, however, would venture to say that *all authoritarian parents are by definition emotionally neglectful.*

Many authoritarian parents tend to equate the child's obedience with love. In other words, if the child quietly and thoroughly obeys the parent, the parent feels loved. Unfortunately, the converse is also true. If the child questions the parent's demand, the parent feels not only disrespected but also rejected. If the child blatantly disobeys, the parent feels all of that plus more. He also feels thoroughly unloved. To understand how this works, let's look in on Sophia.

SOPHIA

Sophia is a beautiful, vivacious 19-year-old woman. Her 62-year-old father is old-school Italian. He loves his only child fiercely, and he expects respect and love from her in return. It is Christmas Eve, and Sophia's family is gathering for the annual Christmas party. Sophia has despised this party for years, as she has no siblings or cousins her age, and she perceives her aunts and uncles as "boring, stuffy and pretentious." At these parties, she feels like an ornament on display. She is presented and evaluated by all the family, and then dismissed and ignored.

This year, Sophia is invited to go to her new boyfriend's house for Christmas Eve with his family. She's excited about the prospect of meeting his parents for the first time and what this means for the relationship moving forward. Also, she feels it will be a much warmer, interesting and exciting way to spend this special night.

When Sophia, with great trepidation, tells her father of her plan, he becomes enraged. "You cannot disrespect me this way. What will your aunts and uncles think? They'll think you don't love them. Is this how you show appreciation for all I've done for you? All I ask is one dinner one time a year, and you're too selfish even to deliver that." When Sophia doesn't immediately fold to his wishes, her father tells her not to bother coming over on Christmas Day. "I'll be returning your gifts, and you can spend Christmas Day with your boyfriend too." At this point,

Sophia feels so guilty and bereft that she agrees to change her plan and follow her father's wishes. She can't bear the thought of spending Christmas Day alone.

Sophia's father responded so harshly because he felt completely spurned and utterly unloved by his daughter. Her willful breaking of his rules was experienced as rejection, disrespect and a lack of caring, whereas it was actually driven by three healthy and positive things: her love for her boyfriend, her excitement about the future, and her natural and normal need to start building her own life. In effect, Sophia's father is inadvertently "training" her to put her own healthy needs aside in order to fulfill his need to feel loved.

JOSEPH

Joseph is ten, the oldest of five siblings, and today is Halloween. Every Halloween of Joseph's short life, the family has followed the same ritual. They have hot dogs and beans at 6:00 p.m. After dinner, the children are finally allowed to don their costumes, although they have been begging to do so since the morning.

Each year Joseph's mother and grandmother choose a theme for the costumes and sew them themselves. This year, all 5 children are Power Rangers. Joseph, being the oldest, is embarrassed, because he feels he has outgrown Power Rangers. He is worrying about his friends seeing him in such a babyish costume and teasing him about it at school tomorrow. Also, he really wanted to be Harry Potter this year. Joseph would never question the costume choice or ask his mother to be Harry Potter, however, because he knows this would make his mother very angry with him for not appreciating the hard work she and his grandmother put into sewing the costumes. So Joseph tries hard not to think about the costume. He puts it out of his mind, and is able to be excited to trick-or-treat despite being a Power Ranger.

Joseph's parents are very strict about the trick-or-treating process. The children are allowed to go to the same seven houses in their neighborhood every year. They are to walk in order of age, youngest first, so that their mother can keep track of them. While walking down the street between houses, Joseph spots two friends down the street trick-or-treating together and impulsively runs ahead, waving and yelling their names. Joseph's mother, who is trying to keep track of all five children and keep order, reacts immediately, grabbing his arm and jerking him back to the end of the line, where he belongs. "No more trick-or-treating for you tonight," she admonishes. "Since you can't control yourself, you can stand back with me while your brothers and sisters go to the rest of the houses. Maybe that will help you remember to behave yourself next year."

Joseph's mother provides a good example of the authoritarian parent. She did not consider Joseph's (or, for that matter, any of the children's) age in deciding the costume and treated all five children as if they were the same age. She was not interested in what Joseph wanted to be for Halloween, finding it easier to make five identical costumes. Her rules are strict and unbending and when Joseph unwittingly breaks them, the consequence is harsh.

We could give Joseph's mom a bit of a pass considering that she had 5 young children to keep track of while trick-or-treating. It could be that her authoritarian ways are based on a desperate attempt to manage five small children. It's important to note, though, that whatever the reasons for her behaviors, they will still have the same effect on Joseph. He is learning that having needs and wishes is selfish and that he's to keep his wishes, needs, and feelings to himself. He's also learning that he is not important. When Joseph enters adolescence, he will be at higher risk of rebellious behavior, and as an adult, he will be very likely to have signs of Emotional Neglect.

Some authoritarian parenting comes in a more subtle package:

RENEE

Renee told me in one of our first therapy sessions, "I was a difficult child. I was always getting into trouble. When I look back, I feel sorry for my parents." When I asked Renee more about this, here's what I learned:

Renee's father was "somewhat of a stickler" (Renee's words). He expected his children to help around the house. He would often come home from work and notice that, for example, the kitchen floor was dirty. "Renee, come and mop this floor!" he would yell. If Renee was in the middle of her homework, she would, very reasonably, try to finish writing her sentence or her arithmetic problem before jumping up. This brief delay was interpreted by her father as disobedience. "When I say come mop the floor, I mean NOW, not 5 minutes from now!" he would yell. This was the case no matter what the task and no matter what Renee was doing at the time her father yelled for her. Needless to say, Renee was often "in trouble."

You might notice that Renee's father did not give her such a strict punishment as some of the other authoritarian parents. He didn't ground her or banish her from Christmas. In fact, what he did would be considered normal by many people's standards. What parent doesn't yell at times? The problem with Renee's dad was that his yelling was loud, and it was mean. It was powered by the *feeling* that his daughter, by not reacting immediately to his demand, did not love him. He was trying to get his needs met (the need to feel respected and loved) and convey to Renee that she'd better do as he says.

Unfortunately, what he actually did was convey to her that her needs were not only inconsequential but also offensive. Renee blamed herself for having unacceptable needs rather than her father for being unreasonable. She was essentially being sentenced to a lifetime of self-blame and self-directed anger. Fortunately, Renee found her way to therapy where she was able to learn to accept that it is okay for her to have her own feelings and needs.

ZEKE

Zeke rides the school bus home with visions of tomorrow's football game dancing in his head. His father was finally able to get Patriots tickets and is taking Zeke to one of their games for the first time. Zeke has never been more excited!

As soon as Zeke arrives home, he hands his mother the note. As she reads it, her face takes on an expression of devastated hurt mixed with anger. "This is unacceptable. You need to learn how to show proper respect! You don't deserve to go to the football game tomorrow. Maybe next time you'll remember to respect Mrs. Rollo."

Obviously Zeke's mother has cracked down hard. She took no time to hear his version of events or to teach him anything about how to manage his emotions or function in a school environment. In place of all of that, she's taught him that as a rule, *he* doesn't matter. All that matters is respecting authority by following it blindly. Even as Zeke grows up and hopefully gets the message from other people in other situations (a teacher, a friend, his wife) that *he does* matter, he will still carry a deep-seated tendency to blame himself when things go wrong, and also to be very hard on himself when he makes a mistake.

Type 3: The Permissive Parent

The permissive parent could be considered the polar opposite of the authoritarian in many ways. The permissive parent's motto is "Don't worry, be happy." In our culture, these types of parents are portrayed as

DREAM PARENTS

beloved and quirky. Think of Dharma's hippy parents on *Dharma and Greg*, Homer Simpson, Stewie's mother on *Family Guy*, or Dennis the Menace's pipe-smoking, laid-back dad. The permissive parent could be described as taking the path of least resistance. At best, they just want their children to be happy. At worst, they simply don't want to have to do the work of parenting. Either way, they do not provide their children with limits, structure, or, in adolescence, a strong adult presence against which the child can rebel. Saying "no" takes energy. Forcing one's child to do a chore or task takes energy. Dealing with an angry child takes energy. Being momentarily hated by your child for saying no is painful. The permissive parent finds it easier to do the chores himself than to make the child do them. And to look the other way or make excuses for the child when he gets into trouble.

Permissive parents are often seen as very loving by their children. This is because permissive parents stir up very little conflict with their children. They simply don't say "no" often enough. Many of these parents have great discomfort with conflict in general, and have their own struggles with self-discipline. To help us understand the permissive parenting style, let's look in on Samantha's "idyllic" childhood.

SAMANTHA

Samantha was the envy of the neighborhood. When all the neighbor kids were called in to dinner one by one, Samantha was free to go in last. When Samantha didn't feel like going to school, she was allowed to take a day off by simply requesting it. When Samantha didn't want to go to bed, it wasn't a problem. She was permitted to choose her own bedtime. Samantha's parents believed that children should have complete freedom, and that this would help them grow up to be happy adults. And indeed Samantha was very happy at home. She rarely clashed with her parents, and as she got older, she simply was seldom home.

At school, however, there were problems. Everyone knew that Samantha was very bright and capable of making excellent grades. However, her teachers found her to be quite difficult. They described her as spoiled, undisciplined and underachieving. She had difficulty following rules and was a behavioral problem in class. She tended to miss test days. So, not surprisingly, her grades were well below her potential.

You can see how Samantha, as an adult looking back, would feel that her parents were wonderful. "I never felt anything other than fully supported by them," she said in her first therapy session with me 15 years later. By that point Samantha was working as the manager of a mall clothing store. She was blaming herself for her lack of a college degree. "I had every opportunity," she said. "My parents would have paid for me to go to college, but I threw all that away. I don't understand what's wrong with me." Samantha had no idea that her parents' permissive style had not prepared her for dealing with the requirements of the real world. She was living with a distorted view of her childhood, so had no ability to understand herself or her struggles.

Not all permissive parents are remembered with fondness. As an adult, Audrey, below, had a complete lack of relationship with her parents and a lot of anger at herself. Read on.

AUDREY

Audrey turned thirteen right at the time that her parents were getting divorced. Her mother was fed up with her father's drinking and cheating, and had finally kicked him out. He moved in quickly with another woman, and Audrey was left to live with her mother and younger sister. Audrey's mother immediately met another man, who moved in with them. Audrey's mother was giddily in love and extremely focused on her new relationship.

When Audrey realized that neither of her parents was paying attention to her comings and goings, she was thrilled. She began running with a group of older kids, smoking pot and drinking. Audrey's mother realized that she was seldom home, but this was OK with her because it gave her mother more time with her boyfriend.

When Audrey was caught at school with pot in her jacket pocket, she told her mother she was just holding it for a friend. Her mother readily accepted this explanation, relieved that her child wasn't using pot. It was much easier to accept Audrey's lame defense than put the effort into investigating, watching, and cracking down on the out-of-control Audrey. By the time she was 18, Audrey had had an abortion (unbeknownst to either of her parents), and had failed numerous high school courses despite having a high IQ.

As an adult looking back, Audrey blamed herself for all of these difficulties. Her parents' near-complete absence in her adolescent years fooled her into thinking that her parents had no influence upon her, either positive or negative. Who, then, could be to blame other than herself? It's hard to see that what's NOT THERE can be more important than what IS there. She had no idea that between her absent father and preoccupied mother, no one had taken the time and energy to actually parent her.

Audrey as a teen, and also as an adult, was making a mistake in her thinking that many people make. Remember that Audrey was delighted at age 13 that no one was watching and saying no or making rules for her? Samantha also was pleased to have no rules. It's natural for adolescents to crave freedom. They're trying to forge their identities and to separate from their parents. The important thing to keep in mind is that while adolescents crave freedom, it is not healthy for them to get too much of it. Adolescents need a strong parent against whom they can rebel. They learn how to make good decisions and manage their impulses by bumping up against a parent's rules and consequences. Unfortunately for Audrey, she had none of this.

Another pitfall of having permissive parents: the child doesn't get enough feedback from her parents. She is left to figure out for herself what she can expect from herself: what she's good at, what her weaknesses are, what she should strive for. To understand this better, let's talk about Eli.

ELI

Eli came home from 5th grade with his report card. He had five C's and two D's. His mother opened it, looked at it, and sadly shook her head. "Well, I'm sure you did your best," she said with a sigh. Eli, greatly relieved in the moment, ran outside to play. Despite his relief, though, he had an uneasy feeling running under the surface while he played. "She said I did my best. That means she doesn't think I can do any better."

Since Eli's mother didn't require or expect much from him, he grew up not requiring much from himself. His mother's permissive style made it easy for him to do the minimum amount of work. And her permissive feedback gave him a message that his mother may not even have intended. By taking the path of least resistance, she taught him not to expect or demand much from himself because he's not capable of delivering anyway.

ZEKE

Zeke handed his mother the note. A barely perceptible shadow crossed her face but was quickly replaced by a brightening. She picked up a football that Zeke had left on the kitchen counter earlier, pointed toward the living room and said, "Go long!" Zeke ran to catch the ball. When he caught it, his mom jumped up and down, making cheering noises from the crowd. "You're such a tough guy," she said while mussing his hair. "Rough day though, huh? Would some ice-cream make it better?"

Zeke's mother could easily be interpreted as very loving and caring by anyone who was watching. After all, she wants Zeke to feel better, right? Parents like Zeke's mom are often seen as "the cool parent" by their children's friends. If Zeke's friends had seen his mother react to problems this way, they'd probably envy him. They'd probably see their own parents as strict and boring in comparison. But even though she may be loving and caring, she has failed her child. She's treating Zeke as a buddy, a pal, not like a child who needs rules to live by and help managing his impulses. A loving, caring parent who is able to do the real work of parenting would not give her child the message that the trouble he had at school isn't important or that there's nothing to be learned from his mistakes. Zeke's mother traded the opportunity to teach him some valuable lessons for the opportunity to be his pal.

The reality is that not all permissive parents are parenting this way out of selfishness, as were Audrey's parents. Many permissive parents, like Zeke's mother, love their children very much and have the best of intentions. Often they are simply parenting their children as they themselves were parented. They don't realize that they must be in the role of authority with their child, via limits, consequences, and saying "no," in order to help their child know himself and understand relationships and feelings.

Type 4: The Bereaved Parent: Divorced or Widowed

Bereaved parents are often just desperately trying to cope. It's not easy to have a parent who is grieving. It's even harder when they are grieving your other parent, whom *you* lost *too*. Children who lose a parent through divorce or death have their own grieving to do. Grief in a family can be very complicated and difficult. But in this book, we are interested mainly in just one aspect of this situation: when it results in Emotional Neglect of the child.

SALLY

Sally is the middle of 5 children in a loving Irish family. Every day, Sally's family is busy with church activities, Little League, PTA, neighbors, school, cookouts and piano lessons. The children fight a lot because they're all close in age, but mostly they get along and love each other. Sally's mom is a very busy lady trying to keep up with the children's school and sports while also working part-time at the town Recreation Department. Sally's mom often tells her friends that she's glad to have her part-time job, as it's the only non-mom-related thing in her life, and without it she would lose her mind. Sally's dad is an engineer. He makes a good living, and life hurries along with little financial concern.

Sally's mother and father have very different temperaments. Her mom tends to be often overwhelmed, distracted and exhausted with the demands of her children. Her father is not home a lot because he works hard and has a commute, but when he is home, he enjoys his children. As middle children sometimes do, Sally tends to get somewhat overlooked in the family. She's not the oldest or the youngest or the only girl or the most talented. But she has a secret feeling that she is her father's favorite daughter. When they were having their family picture taken, he asked Sally to sit on his lap. Sometimes on Sunday mornings, she gets to sit next to him, and they read the comics together

When Sally was eight years old, she heard her parents talking in hushed whispers. She tried to listen but could only make out a few words. One word she did hear was "cancer." Sally didn't want to think about that, so she ran off to play. Gradually over the next few months she noticed her father losing weight. Six months later, he stopped working and stayed in bed all day. The day he didn't go to work, the parents had a family meeting and told the children that their father had cancer. "But everything will be OK," they said. "We don't want you kids to worry about this."

Three months later Sally came home from school, threw her books on the kitchen table and went to the fridge for a glass of milk. Her older sister came into the room with a tear-streaked face and said, "Daddy's gone. They took him away." Over the course of the next several months, the full gravity of that statement would hit Sally. She saw her mother very little for the first week after her father disappeared, and when she did see her, her face was still, as if carved from stone. Sally's mother spoke little, and did not mention Sally's father or the loss of him. She did not talk directly about it to any of her children. She let the helpful neighbors, aunts and uncles care for the children, with instructions to try to keep their lives as normal as possible. So Sally was driven to her piano lesson and taken to watch her brother's baseball game. The only day they were held back from school was the day of the funeral. On that day, the children were dressed up, driven to the church for the funeral and driven home. Still, no one spoke about her father's death. Sally was afraid to say anything to her mother or ask any questions because she had the feeling that any wrong question could make her mother's stone face crumble. Sally didn't want to hurt her mother.

After the funeral, life went on. It went on as if nothing at all had happened. No one mentioned Sally's father. It was if he had never existed. But the family's life changed drastically. Sally's mother had to get a full-time job working in a cafeteria. They sold their house and moved into a much smaller rented apartment with no yard. Sally's mother was gone 9 hours a day at her job. When she was home, she was almost always doing chores, and often with that stone face on. Sally learned to steer clear of her mother, because any need she had seemed to push her mother close to the edge. Sally lived in fear of seeing her mother fall apart.

When I first met Sally at the age of 40, she was single, never married. She was a successful biotech engineer with a house of her own, a dog and a passion for Sudoku puzzles. But Sally came to therapy because she wasn't happy. "I haven't been happy since I was eight years old," she said. Although she functioned just fine and had made a place for herself in the world, for 32 years she had struggled with a sadness that she couldn't shake and an empty feeling that she couldn't escape. Sally once told me, "Other people live in a different world from me. They see colors, feel things, love each other and get excited. I have none of that. To me, the world is gray. I'm on the outside, looking in."

Sally was right. She really was living in a gray world. She was running on a half-empty tank of low-octane fuel that had been diluted by a pool of unshed tears. Here are some of the feelings that Sally had been holding inside all those years:

- shock over her father's sudden disappearance from her life
- grief over the loss of him
- anger that she hadn't been told that her father was going to die
- fear of talking about anything feeling-related because it might hurt another person (this message she had taken from her mom's stone face)
- loss of the feeling of being "special," as she never again felt like she was anyone's favorite
- fear of becoming attached again since, from her experience, attachment is disastrously painful
- anger at her family and herself for pretending that her father had never existed after his death
- guilt that she had sometimes wished, periodically throughout her life, that it had been her mother, instead of her father, who had died.

It's important to note here that Sally's mother was a good woman. She worked hard and did her best, despite being overwhelmed. When she learned of her husband's illness and that he was going to die and eventually lost him, she did not have the tools to manage her own grief herself, much less to communicate about it with her children. She went into Survival Mode, and coped with the "head down, nose to the grindstone" technique. She did the best she could possibly do with the tools she had available to her. Part of Sally's work was to try to understand why and how it had all unfolded this way, how it had affected her, and all of the intense feelings she had internalized and buried as a result.

In our work together Sally was eventually able to uncover each and every one of those feelings. She spent many hours in my office shedding the tears that she had been holding outside of her awareness all these years. Sally was able, through a lot of hard work, to start to tune in to herself, feel alive, and see the world's colors as others do.

ZEKE

Zeke comes home from school feeling nervous that he has to show his father the note. He wishes he could hand it to his mother, but this is Thursday, and he always spends Thursday nights with his dad since his parents got divorced. Zeke knows his dad will not take this well because his Dad has been tired, irritable and short-tempered since Zeke's mom moved out. Zeke doesn't understand why his dad has to be this way. His mom and new stepfather seem really happy, and it pains him to see that his dad is not happy too.

Zeke hands his father the note. He watches nervously as his father slowly shakes his head from side to side. "This is your mother's fault," he says. "I'm not surprised that you're starting to get into trouble after all that she's put us through. Don't worry, I'll definitely talk to her about this."

You might imagine that Zeke would be confused by his father's reaction. Zeke's own impulses and feisty nature are completely overlooked by his dad, who chooses to see the situation as ammunition to use against his ex-wife, who left him precipitously and remarried quickly. Zeke may be relieved that he's off the hook, but deep down he feels overlooked. His dad attempts to seem like he's being protective of Zeke, but in reality he's advancing his own agenda. Sadly, Zeke has no opportunity to learn anything from his mistake.

It's certainly understandable for a man to feel angry and hurt when he's suddenly left by his wife. It's also understandable for him to worry that this might damage the child they have together. When Zeke looks back on this scenario from the vantage point of adulthood, he'll remember clearly how his dad was protective and didn't get angry with him for getting in trouble. What Zeke *won't remember* is what *didn't happen.* And what didn't happen was all of the things the mother did in my example of emotionally attuned parenting. You may recall that it involves knowing the child's feelings, talking with the child, setting limits and giving the child a rule to live by. If Zeke's dad continues to ignore his feelings and needs in this way, Zeke will most likely grow up to feel that his dad doesn't really know him as a person at all. But he won't understand the reasons for that because he can't remember what didn't happen. Probably he will blame himself.

Type 5: The Addicted Parent

When we hear the word "addict," most of us think "alcoholic" or "drug addict." But addiction encompasses a much broader range of compulsive behaviors, from gambling, shopping, and internet or porn addictions to scratch tickets, cigarettes, slot machines, and online gaming, to name a few. Some of these activities, pursued in moderation, are pleasant stress relievers. But these pursuits can cross the line into addiction when a person begins to:

- feel intense pleasure–bordering on relief when doing the activity or anticipating doing it
- spend more and more time on the activity, so that family members notice or complain
- spend money and other resources on the activity, whether or not one can afford it
- use the activity for many purposes: to relieve stress, socialize, play, manage emotions or entertain others
- deny that the activity is harming oneself or anyone else

In an unprecedented boom of high-tech toys, credit purchases, unlimited web access, and social networking, there's plenty of potential for any of us to develop an addiction. Americans, in particular, are used to high stress and immediate gratification, both of which feed addictions.

Most recently, neuroscientist David Linden wrote about the range of pleasures that our brains may become addicted to. He urges the reader to view addicts compassionately, the way you would any other ill person. But what makes that difficult for family members is the harm that the addict invariably causes the people closest to him.

Addicted parents are not all the same. At one end of the spectrum there is a father or mother who is lost to drugs or alcohol and experiences obvious consequences. Children of these dysfunctional addicted parents are not only emotionally neglected, but traumatized. This is not the parent we're discussing here. We're interested in the functional, loving parent whose addiction may not even be identified as a problem in the family. These are the parents about whom my clients say some variation of "He had his beers every night, but it wasn't a problem." These are the parents who are forgiven for the wine every night, even if they get irritable or mushy, because they are there for their children in many ways. Functional addicted parents are capable of being good parents. They are there at the football game with the cooler and the snacks for the team. They invite over your cousins and aunts and uncles and have barbecues. When you get in trouble at school, they can march into the principal's office and stick up for you. They can make you laugh.

So what can a loving soccer mom who likes her wine possibly have done or not done to wind up in this book? Or a hardworking father who likes to bet on every sport on television? Are they guilty of emotionally neglectful parenting? Simply put, what harms children of functional, addicted parents is this: they are behaving like two people. And the child cannot always predict which side of her addicted parent is going to show up. When caught up in their addicted behavior, they forget to parent. They are temporarily asleep on the job, and so can be mean, frightening, immature, selfish or inappropriate. When not caught up in the behavior, the same parent can be kind, supportive, wise, helpful, fun or reassuring. So for the child of a functionally addicted parent, memories of family life are invariably mixed, with positive memories interspersed with sad ones. After a childhood chock full of unpredictable parenting, the adult child of the addict is anxious, worried and secretly insecure.

RICHARD

Richard comes to therapy at age 27 after experiencing a few panic attacks at work. He hadn't known what they were, and ended up in the ER twice thinking he was having a heart attack. His father is a highly respected fire chief. When asked, Richard tells me that he had been a star baseball player as a teen. In his junior year of high school he was even nominated for MVP of the year. Richard also proudly tells me that his father came to every single one of his games. He remembers that his dad often pitched so that he could have batting practice. So far, so good, right?

Later in my session with Richard, I ask, "Was there ever a time you can remember growing up when you felt very, very anxious, similar to what you've been experiencing lately?" Here is what he tells me: "It was the awards banquet at the end of the baseball season, junior year. It was at 8pm and I had a little concern because Dad usually had had a few beers by then. When my name wasn't called as the season's MVP, and my teammate got it, my dad just stood up and said in his booming fire chief voice, "That damn kid doesn't deserve it. My son made All-State!" Everyone stopped in shock, looking from me to my dad and back to me again. I was mortified. I just stumbled out of there, went outside and threw up. I don't like to think about that memory. By the spring of the next season, I was partying too much to play baseball."

Children of addicted parents experience the lack of predictability as highly anxiety-provoking. As adults, they are therefore at significantly higher risk to have anxiety disorders and to become addicts themselves than are people who were raised by non-addicted parents. Being a good parent most of the time and a horrible parent once in awhile creates insecure, anxious adults who are just waiting for things to go wrong.

Another aspect of addicted parenting that amounts to Emotional Neglect is the addicted parent's tendency to balance his periods of neglect with periods of control and intrusiveness:

ELSIE

Elsie is a dark-eyed, insightful 12-year-old brought to therapy by her mother. Her mother, Catherine, is addicted to being thin and also abuses alcohol. She complains to the therapist about Elsie, saying that her grades have gone down and that she has become disrespectful and "mopey." She calls Elsie an "overly-dramatic princess." Elsie's father travels a lot on business, and it is mostly Elsie, her mom and her younger sister at home. When her mother leaves Elsie and me alone in my office for our first appointment, Elsie tells me that she loves her mother, but that she wouldn't "pick someone like her for a friend, because she can be mean." She says that the minute she puts her hand on the front doorknob of her house after school she gets a worried feeling. If her mother hasn't yet poured a glass of wine, things are fine. But if she has, she usually gives Elsie the evil eye when Elsie goes to get a snack or gets on Elsie to go out and exercise (even though Elsie is thin). Sometimes, says Elsie, it helps to have a mom who watches what she eats. But even though her mom tells her that she isn't fat, Elsie believes that when her mom says "That crap you're eating is fattening," or "That's enough," or "Go ride your bike, you lazy girl," or "Those pants look tight," she means that Elsie doesn't measure up. When she isn't drinking, however, Elsie's mom would not say anything like that.

When parents are caught up in their own addictions, they aren't capable of noticing their child's emotions; nor can they relate to their child as he or she really is. When Elsie's mom, under the influence of alcohol, would tell Elsie "Go ride your bike, you lazy girl," for example, she was not truly talking about Elsie. She was actually expressing her own feelings about herself (her fear of being fat). When not under the influence, she was able to see Elsie realistically and tell her so. But after a glass of wine, everything was different. This is a perfect example of Emotional Neglect in action. Elsie is treated as a non-person, simply a reflection of how her mother sees herself. Unfortunately, being a child, Elsie had no idea that this was happening. She took her mother's comments to heart, and by the time I met her, she had low self-esteem and a longstanding feeling of not being good enough.

ZEKE

Zeke gets off the school bus feeling anxious. He wonders what he can do to kill some time before he has to go home and give his mother the note from his teacher. He knows that if he can just get home a little later, his mom might be already absorbed in her computer game and not give the note much attention. Zeke's not afraid of his mother's reaction. But he's a bright child, and has figured out over time that he can sometimes get away with things when his mom's absorbed with the computer. So Zeke walks around the block, stops by his friend Scott's house, and takes some time looking for cool rocks in the neighbor's driveway. After a while, he realizes if he doesn't get home soon his mom might get worried, so he gathers up all of his courage and walks in the front door.

Zeke notices immediately, with a sigh of relief, that his mother doesn't look up at him when he arrives. "How was school?" she calls to him. "OK. I brought you a note from my teacher," Zeke replies. Zeke briskly plants the note on his mom's computer desk and runs into the kitchen to look for cookies. He knows his mom won't stop her game to look at it, and by the time she's finished she may have forgotten it's there. With a sigh of relief at the success of his Operation Put Off Getting Into

Trouble As Long As Possible, he hopes that she wins her games today so she'll be in a good mood and won't be upset even if she does end up seeing the note.

It's important to take note that Zeke is not really worried that his mother will overreact or become angry or abusive. His mother is actually kind, reasonable and loving. The issue here is that his mother's computer addiction opens a window for him. He has quickly and easily learned how to use that window to avoid things, including the consequences of his own behavior. If he's able to use it on something as serious as a note from his teacher, we can probably safely assume that he's used it in many smaller situations.

Zeke has been emotionally neglected here in that his issue at school may fall between the cracks due to his mother's addiction. If he is successful in his Operation, he will not be called to explain himself, he will not get the feeling of being understood. He will not learn how to recognize or put words to his own emotions. In contrast, the things he will learn from his addicted mother are how to avoid consequences and how to "play" people. Interestingly, as an adult Zeke will probably not recall this incident of the note from his teacher at all. If he does, it's very likely that he will blame himself for being manipulative, but not his mother for emotionally neglecting him. He'll recall what he himself *did*, not what his mother *didn't do*.

Type 6: The Depressed Parent

Let's revisit third-grader Zeke, who we just left above, but he will have a depressed parent this time:

ZEKE

On his way home on the bus, Zeke feels terrible that he got into trouble at school. He knows that his dad is probably home on the couch where he's spent a lot of time since he lost his job.

When Zeke walks through the door, he sees that he was right. His father is lying on the couch with his eyes closed, with ESPN Sport Center providing a lively backdrop. Zeke greets his dad and hands him the note. He adores his father and doesn't understand why he doesn't do anything anymore. His father reads the note and a look of pain crosses his face. His dad sighs. "Don't do it again, okay, Zeke? That's no way to behave." Zeke is flooded with shame, realizing that it is HIS poor behavior that makes dad sad. "I won't, Dad," he mumbles. He stands there for a moment longer, but his dad closes his eyes and appears to go back to his nap. Zeke quietly retreats.

If his depressed father doesn't get some help, the outlook for Zeke isn't good. He will grow up feeling that he must be a perfectly behaved child so as not to make his dad feel worse. This pattern may become entrenched in his personality, so that he has great difficulty rocking the boat, making mistakes or allowing himself to be an imperfect human being.

The depressed parent has little energy or enthusiasm for the job of parenting. Unlike the narcissistic parent who demands attention, the depressed parent often seems to disappear. He is turned inward, focused on himself and what's wrong with him, worried about whether he's going to make it. He has low energy and little to give. He is missing in action in the lives of his family. And when he *is* present, he may be irritable or glum. In the face of this, children who are growing up with depressed parents don't know how to get attention from adults in positive ways. Good behavior goes unnoticed, while misbehavior commands at least some attention, however negative it may be.

The results of this type of Emotional Neglect are well documented. In school, children of depressed parents are more likely to be perceived as troublemakers than children of non-depressed parents. Because the depressed parent offers little comfort or encouragement, his child doesn't know how to self-soothe and may turn to drugs or alcohol in adolescence. Because depressed parents appear put-upon, beleaguered or overwhelmed by the ordinary demands of parenting, their children don't always learn that they are worthwhile and so are at risk to become depressed themselves in adulthood. Finally, because depressed parents have inadequate control over their own behavior, their children are at risk to be out of control themselves.

MARGO

Margo thinks she's a real badass. At 16, she was kicked out of her public high school for drinking in the girl's bathroom and procuring weed for her softball team. She is being tutored at home. She has told her parents that she has absolutely no intention of stopping partying. When her parents make half-hearted attempts to set limits, she usually walks out the door and goes to a friend's house. Margo tells her friends' mothers all about how awful her own parents are to her, so they are sympathetic to her. Unfortunately, Margo's parents are too apathetic to follow up with other parents, so Margo's description of their alleged atrocities stands. At home, Margo stays in her room and video chats with men on Skype. She shocks her friends by telling them about her daring video sexting episodes.

Margo's parents, Elaine and Bruce, are good people. They give to charity, belong to a church, and are kind and respectful to all. But each of Margo's parents is depressed in a different way. They are a little older than her friends' parents, having adopted Margo after years of futile fertility treatments. They have lots of money, thanks to a substantial amount of early Microsoft stock. But Elaine hadn't ever gotten over the 14 years spent trying to become pregnant. Margo frequently finds her mother on the couch when she comes home, sometimes still in pajamas. This enrages Margo, and at such times she is contemptuous and provocative toward her mom. Her dad is not much more involved with Margo. He feels empty and without purpose since he stopped working. He goes to the library and takes courses to pass the time. Margo can remember fun times with him when she was little, but he has become more remote since his wife has gotten more depressed. Often, he brings home take-out since Elaine doesn't cook much. But then he just sits beside Margo's mother in his recliner, watching TV and nodding off.

Starting around 8th grade, Margo used to think a lot about how sad and regretful her parents would be at her funeral if she died. Imagining her parents and friends grieving helped in some way when she was sad. These thoughts became so frequent that she started thinking about killing herself for real. When she overdosed and ended up in the ER and then a psych hospital, her parents seemed to wake up and pay attention to her. Lately, they tell her they love her and ask her if she feels safe at bedtime, like the psychologist has told them to do. They are worried about her and question her every time she stays in her room too long. As far as Margo is concerned, finally getting some attention paid to her is great! But Margo is afraid if she gets too happy, they'll stop worrying and go back to being the way they were before. She thinks she sees it happening already.

You might be glad to know that Margo's parents did not, in fact, go back to being emotionally distant and depressed. They all got help, and healing for Margo is underway.

Not all households with depressed parents are as extreme as Zeke's or Margo's. But when the depressed parent's toxic mix of inattention and distance continues for any length of time, the result is Emotional Neglect of the developing child.

Type 7: The Workaholic Parent

Workaholism is often seen as a positive in our society. The TV show 30 Rock portrays the workaholic quite well in the character of super

"Just wait until your nanny gets here."

ambitious businessman Jack Donaghy (played by Alec Baldwin). In one funny scene, lying in his hospital bed after barely surviving a work-stress-induced heart attack, he says with great feeling, "Being so close to death has shown me that I've lived my life all wrong." When Tina Fey's character leans in close to better hear the wisdom he's about to impart, he whispers weakly, "I should have worked *longer* hours, and put *more* into my job."

In our capitalist economy, we value hard work and high salaries. Of all the addictions mentioned above (for example alcohol, drugs, shopping or gambling), work is the only one that actually brings money *into* the household. Workaholics are often driven, successful people who are admired and looked up to by co-workers, family and community. Unfortunately, it's their children who often suffer in silence. Workaholic parents work long hours, are obsessed by their jobs, and tend to pay inadequate attention to the needs and feelings of their children. To make matters worse, children of workaholics garner little sympathy from others, as they often have successful parents, plenty of money, and nice things. By putting their work first, workaholics convey the message to their children that their feelings and needs are of lesser importance (damaging their children's self-worth). By failing to be an active part of their children's accomplishments and triumphs, they inadvertently convey a message that those accomplishments don't matter (damaging their children's self-esteem). Some children act out in school or with alcohol and drugs to get their parents' attention. Others grow up with inadequate self-worth, low self-esteem, and no understanding of how they got this way. Since they view themselves as privileged, not deprived, they blame themselves for their inner struggles. Low self-worth, low self-esteem, and self-blame quickly add up to depression.

SAM

When Sam first came to me for therapy at age 19, he was in his freshman year at a very expensive private college, and he was very depressed. He was failing out of college due to the great difficulty he was experiencing in getting himself out of bed in the morning. He often lost the battle, spending all day sleeping and missing his classes altogether. He was disgusted with himself and expressed it to me this way: "I'm pathetic. My parents have worked so hard to give me a better life than they had, and they've given me every advantage. Here I am throwing it all away, and I have no excuse for it."

In order to understand what was going on with Sam, you must first understand his parents. Sam's parents met in high school and married at age 19. They both came from uneducated, impoverished families. Although both were quite bright, neither had the opportunity to go to college due to their financial situations. From the moment they married, they knew they would have to work very hard to make a decent life for themselves and their children. Sam's father worked his way up from construction worker to managing jobsites all over the country. Although this required him to travel frequently, his salary jumped far beyond anything he had ever imagined. In the meantime, Sam's mother started out working the front desk at a chain hotel. She also worked her way up, eventually becoming Executive Assistant to the CEO of the company, and also commanding a very impressive salary. Unfortunately, part of her job was to jump when the CEO said jump. This meant frequent middle-of-the-night calls, meetings extending well into the late evening, and spur-of-the-moment business travel. The bigger Sam's parents' jobs became the more excited and invested in them his parents became. They were achieving far beyond their wildest dreams, and it hadn't occurred to them that they could stop, or even cut back.

As his parents' jobs grew over the years, Sam gradually lost his parents. Sam, his parents, and everyone else talked frequently about how lucky Sam was as they kept replacing their houses with bigger ones and buying nicer cars. When he was 9, his parents hired his first nanny. Everyone could see what Sam was gaining materially, but his gradual loss of his parents was invisible to everyone. Between the ages of 9 and 19, Sam went from a child with two loving, attentive parents to a college student who was raised by a nanny and was now expected to thrive at college.

Everyone knows that if a child's parent dies, the child will suffer with sadness, loss, and possibly depression. No one thinks about this being the case when a child loses a parent to success. Since Sam had no conscious awareness of his loss of his parents, he had no understanding of his sadness and symptoms of depression. He naturally assumed that he had brought it upon himself. That set him up for a lot of self-anger, self-blame and low self-worth as a teen, and later as an adult.

ZEKE

> *Zeke walked in the door of his beautiful, spacious home and handed the note to his father, who had stopped by to change clothes before going to an evening meeting. His mother was away traveling for business. His father peered over his reading glasses at Zeke with a disappointed look. "This is not good Zeke. I'm sorry I have to rush to my meeting right now, but I'm going to give this note to Trish (the nanny) and she'll talk with you about it tonight."*

You may be wondering what's so bad about this scenario. After all Zeke has a beautiful home, an obviously caring but busy father, and a nanny who attends to him. But sadly, the reality is that even if the nanny is a wonderful and tuned-in caretaker who says all the right things as she interacts with Zeke, this will still constitute Emotional Neglect. Because Zeke's dad passes the issue to the nanny he gives Zeke the message loud and clear that his dad's job is more important than Zeke's own life lessons. Later, Zeke will likely remember these things that *happened*: his father's not-unkind reaction, his nanny's talk with him, and perhaps even what he learned from it. He will not realize or remember that his father wasn't able to take time away from his job to talk to him about the note himself, or of the "less-than" message he received from his father that day. Instead, he'll very possibly be prone to low self-worth. He has the opportunity to process and understand events that *happened*, but he has no chance to process what he can't remember *what didn't happen*.

Type 8: The Parent with a Special Needs Family Member

There is no category of parent who deserves to be in a book about Emotional Neglect LESS than the parent in a household where someone is ill or severely impaired. Yet here they are, through no fault of their own, because life has delivered a challenge which is often unmanageable. Listen in on the conversation that parents Tom and Patty are having with their daughter, Miranda, age 13, the youngest of 3 children.

"You are such a big help to us, Miranda" says her dad, Tom.

"You sure are!" adds Patty. "I know it's been especially hard lately with Patrick back at Children's Hospital having his new shunt put in. Your brother Steven does nothing but complain. But you! You're my rock!"

And here is what it sounds like in the Smith household, where 10 year-old Jack's older brother suffers from behavioral and emotional problems associated with autism:

"I know it's frustrating that Todd takes your stuff," Jack's dad tells him. "I know it's hard to listen to him freaking out so much lately since his meds were changed. I'm sorry our basketball game was interrupted, but your Mom needed my help with Todd. You deserve better. But you know Jack, for now we all just have to be good to each other and be patient. Todd can't help his problems. Your Mom and I are doing the best we can. It'll get better."

And finally, here's what goes on in Zeke's household:

Zeke comes in through the kitchen and the screen door slams. He enters the house with dread, because he knows he'll have to show his mom the note from his teacher. Zeke feels awful because here is another burden for his mother to have to deal with, when she's already dealing with so much. Quickly, Zeke's mother appears from another part of the house, her finger pressed to her lips. "Shhh, Zeke! Your father is asleep. He had a rough night last night." At first, Zeke feels a giant wave of relief. He had hoped that his father would be asleep so that he'd only have to deal with his mother's reaction to the note. But the relief is quickly replaced by shame. "My father is sick and all I care about is myself. I'm a bad person."

When a child grows up with a serious illness in the family, whether it's that of a parent or of a sibling, the care-giving that would normally go toward the child is compromised. Tom, Jack and Zeke don't have the freedom to be themselves. Notice that Zeke feels guilty for having normal events and feelings (having a note sent home and hoping to avoid trouble for it).

Often, the caregiver parent is stretched thin herself and calls upon the well child–implicitly or explicitly–to selflessly help out. Life in a household with an ill child or parent is often in crisis mode. For example, while a parent makes frequent trips to the hospital, the emotionally neglected child heats a frozen dinner and eats alone in front of the TV. Or the child finds himself constantly catching bits of medical conversations he wasn't supposed to hear and doesn't understand. The child gets rides with someone else's parents to soccer games. He gets used to his parents being irritated by him for little reason.

Parents of ill households usually recognize that there is an impact on the healthy child. They may check in with him, attempt to discuss how he's doing and offer what support they can. They are conscious of the amount of time spent on the ill family member, and even worry about it. So these parents seem like the last parents who would emotionally neglect their healthy children. But multiple studies have examined the perceptions of both the parents and the healthy child in a household where someone is ill. In these studies, the parents and the healthy child are asked to rate how the healthy child is doing. Results consistently show that parents see their healthy child as doing "okay," while that same child perceives him or herself in a much more negative light. Conclusions? When parents are (or feel) powerless to change the bad things in their children's lives, they tend to minimize the effects of those bad things. Not only do such parents subconsciously minimize their child's distress, they also inadvertently burden him with a maturity of which he is not really capable. They often need and expect their healthy child to be as compassionate, as selfless and as patient as they themselves need to be.

Sometimes, family illnesses impact an entire childhood. In such cases, the child is likely to develop quasi-adult behaviors that don't fall apart until adolescence:

STUART

Stuart's father and mother bring him to therapy because, they say, at age 15 he has become "so negative." Initially, he is almost silent for several meetings, resenting that he has been forced to come here, and refusing to say much. I see immediately that Stuart's parents are consumed by concern for Stuart's older brother, Larry, who has a disease that makes him extremely vulnerable to infections. I see this because while attempting to take Stuart's developmental history in the parent interview, Stuart's parents keep drifting back to the subject of Larry, and are seemingly unaware of doing it. From that, I know that Stuart, like many siblings of ill children, has held in his negative emotions and his own needs for years.

It seems clear to me that Stuart has finally reached his breaking point. His facade is crumbling, and he can no longer be "okay." The breakdown of Stuart's stoic attitude is inevitable but mysterious to his parents. They wonder where their helpful, nice son has gone and they've brought him to therapy to "fix" his negative attitude.

After a few meetings alone with me, Stuart begins to talk. He explains to me that he doesn't bring friends home because he feels guilty that he can have normal friendships while Larry cannot. And he's also wary that his friends might not understand some of Larry's quirky behaviors. And then he feels guilty for being embarrassed by his brother, whom he loves.

So here he is in my office, feeling guilty for causing his parents more problems, starved for attention, resentful that they can't recognize his sorrow, and unable to put any of it into words. When, after a few meetings, Stuart has an incident at home in which he gets verbally angry with them, his parents tell me that therapy is "making Stuart worse." I encourage Stuart to respond and he blurts out, "Everything is always about Larry. You even left my All-Star game early to pick up his

> *medications!" His parents start to protest, saying they left just a few minutes early and that he's being overly sensitive. At this point, I intervene firmly: "This is exactly the problem. Stuart isn't really allowed to say how he feels. And when he does, you call him sensitive. Larry is not the only child who needs help. But your good intentions for helping Larry are interfering with your ability to parent Stuart. You're making him feel guilty for having needs and feelings."*

This difficult moment in my office was a turning point for Stuart. Luckily, these parents were ultimately able to understand how Larry's illness had stunted Stuart's social and emotional growth for quite some time, causing him to hold in guilt, anger and sadness. Although they brought Stuart to therapy in hopes that *he* would change, it turned out that *their* change was as dramatic as Stuart's, if not more so.

The reason they had failed to notice Stuart struggling was that he'd given them no trouble growing up. Stuart's parents finally realized that that's what they'd been expecting from him throughout his brother's illness, no trouble. With this awareness, Stuart's parents began to pay more attention to his needs and feelings. If they are able to continue that throughout Stuart's adolescence, the effects of Emotional Neglect can be reversed, and Stuart can grow up to be happy and healthy.

Type 9: The Achievement/ Perfection Focused Parent

The Achievement/Perfection Focused Parent seldom seems to be satisfied. If his child comes home with straight A's, he will say, "Next time I'll expect A+'s." This parent has a few things in common with the Narcissistic Parent we talked about. In fact, many of his behaviors are similar. A lot of Narcissistic parents are perfection-focused because they want their child to reflect well on them. In other words, "If my child makes straight A's, it makes me look really good." This 'mirror effect' is some part of most Achievement/Perfection parents (we'll call them AP

parents for short), but it's not always. AP parents can be motivated by a number of different factors.

Not all AP parents are emotionally neglectful. Many parents of Olympic athletes, concert pianists and professional baseball players could be considered AP because they are driven and they support their child to be the best. But the difference between a non-neglectful AP parent and a neglectful one is this: support. A healthy AP parent is *supporting* her child to achieve what *the child* wants. An unhealthy AP parent is *pressuring* her child to achieve what *the parent* wants.

Some AP parents pressure their children to achieve because they desperately want opportunities for their children that they themselves did not have. Many are acting out of their own feeling that they themselves must be perfect. Some are trying to live their own life through their child. Still other AP parents may be simply raising their child the way they themselves were raised because it's what they know.

When young Zeke hands the note to his AP mom, what do you think she would say?

ZEKE

"Zeke, how could you behave this way at school? Now Mrs. Rollo may change her mind about writing the recommendation letter to help with your application to the Superior Amazing Child School! We need to call Mrs. Rollo right now and smooth this over."

Or AP Mom #2:

"Zeke, you know better than to balance a pencil on your finger point-side-up! Mrs. Rollo is right. If you poked yourself in the eye it could slow down your progress on the piano. How can you practice if you can't see the music?!"

Or AP Mom #3:

"Zeke, I'm terribly disappointed in you. I've made so many sacrifices so that you can be at this expensive school. If Mrs. Rollo starts to see you as a problem child you may ruin everything I've done for you. You have to think about your future!"

Notice that all three of these reactions seem to have Zeke's best interests in mind. These AP mothers are clearly concerned about their child and want the best for him. The problem is that all three mothers are emotionally neglecting Zeke with their responses. None of these responses addresses Zeke's need to learn to control his impulses. None addresses Zeke's recent feelings of being treated like a baby by his siblings. None of these responses talks to Zeke about anything that matters to *him*. All of the responses address the parent's needs, not Zeke's. They address Zeke's future, which he is too young to care about or even understand. They take away an opportunity for Zeke to learn something about himself, his nature, his feelings, and how to get along with authority figures. Over time, in order to take in the simplistic message, "Be good so that you can be successful," Zeke will have to squelch many of his own needs and feelings. This may work fine in childhood, but he will enter adolescence and adulthood with something missing inside; self-knowledge, emotional awareness, and self-love.

TIM

Tim was literally dragged to couple's therapy by his wife, Trish. In our first appointment, it was hard to get Tim to say much at all. The one thing he expressed when he did talk was that he was disappointed in himself and Trish. "We love each other, and that should be enough. But nothing's ever enough for Trish," he said. When I asked him to elaborate, he would only say, "I can't see why she won't just let things go. Why can't she just be happy?"

If I had taken this at face value, I might have been thinking at that point that Trish must be somewhat difficult to get along with. But having worked with many couples, I could see that there was definitely a lot more to the story. As I asked Trish questions, she started to cry. Here's what she told me about her reasons for bringing Tim to therapy.

"Tim says he's happy in our marriage but he doesn't seem happy. He comes home from work irritable. He's a wonderful father, but sometimes he snaps at the kids when they behave any way other than perfect. He's always down on himself. He's a V.P. at his company at only forty years old, but he still feels inadequate because he thinks he should be CEO by now. When I try to talk to him, he shuts me down. I know he's miserable and I want to help but I can't. At this point, I love him but I can't live this way anymore. Please help us so that we can stay together."

Let's pause here for a moment and consider Tim. Already in the first fifteen minutes of our first session, I strongly suspected that he was emotionally neglected as a child. Here were the Emotional Neglect signs that I could see in him (when you read Chapter 3, you'll learn much more about these signs):

- irritability
- perfectionism, evidenced by his lack of tolerance for his kids' mistakes
- lack of emotional awareness, evidenced by "Why can't she just be happy?"
- counter-dependence, evidenced by feeling disappointed in himself for needing help and by his refusal to accept help from Trish
- lack of compassion for himself, evidenced by Trish's report that Tim feels inadequate for being VP instead of CEO.

> *After half a dozen couple's meetings, Tim was finally willing to have some individual sessions. In those meetings, I discovered that Tim's parents, while loving, raised him with one primary goal: to be successful. His stresses, struggles, achievements and abilities in childhood were all seen through the lens of "the future" by his parents. Tim had learned well that his feelings, needs and experiences were not relevant to anything. All that mattered was, "what does this mean for your future?" Tim entered adulthood, married and had his own children with very little knowledge about himself, his emotions, or how to connect with people, including his wife.*

Fortunately, since Tim was able to open up and share all of this with me, we were able to address it. After a number of individual sessions, he was able to apply his newfound self-acceptance, compassion and tolerance to his marriage and children.

When a child is treated by her AP parents as if her feelings and emotional needs don't matter, a deeply personal part of herself is being denied. That part of her becomes like the elephant in the room. No one wants to see or hear from it, yet it's the part of her which is most *her*. The only way that most of these children can adapt, get along and grow in the family is to participate in the denial, and pretend that their emotional self doesn't exist. No wonder neglected children grow up with an empty space in their sense of themselves, their love for themselves, and their ability to emotionally connect to others.

Type 10: The Sociopathic Parent

This will likely be the most surprising Parent Type that I will talk about in this book. Even if you are 100% certain that this category doesn't apply to you, I recommend that you read this section.

Who comes to your mind when you hear the word "sociopath"? Hannibal Lecter? Tony Soprano? Mussolini? These are indeed iconic representations of the concept. But they are the most extreme, dramatic and obvious versions of sociopathy. The kind of sociopath we're interested in is different. This sociopath quite possibly never breaks a law and has never been to jail, is far less obvious but far more commonplace. This sociopath might be your neighbor, your brother, your mother or your father. She or he can hide behind a perfect manicure, an excellent job, charity work or the PTA. Most people would not ever think of this person as a sociopath. In fact, she may have a charisma that draws people to her. She may be admired and appear selfless and kind to many. But deep down, she is not like the rest of us. Sometimes no one can see that something is wrong except the people who are closest to her. Often her children can feel it, but that doesn't mean they understand it.

There is one main feature that sets sociopaths apart from the rest of us. That one thing can be expressed in one word: conscience. Simply put, a sociopath feels no guilt. Because of this, he's freed up to do virtually anything without having to pay any internal price for it. A sociopath can say or do anything she wants and not feel bad the next day, or ever. Along with a lack of guilt comes a profound lack of empathy. For the sociopath, other people's feelings are meaningless because she has no ability to feel them. In fact, sociopaths don't really feel anything the way the rest of us do. Their emotions operate under a very different system, which revolves around controlling others. If the sociopath succeeds in controlling you, he may actually feel some love for you. The flip side of that coin is that if he fails at controlling you, he will despise you. He uses underhanded means to get his way, and if that doesn't work, he'll bully. If that fails, he'll retaliate by trying to hurt you.

Having no conscience frees up the sociopath to use any underhanded means to get her way. She can be verbally ruthless. She can portray things falsely. She can twist others' words to her own purposes. She can blame others when things go awry. It's not necessary to own her mistakes because it's much easier to blame someone else. The sociopath has discovered the value of playing "the victim," and plays it like a virtuoso.

According to Dr. Martha Stout, who wrote *The Sociopath Next Door*, the single most reliable indicator that you're dealing with a sociopath is when a person appears to purposely hurt you and then proceeds normally as if they did nothing wrong, and as if you should not be hurt. If someone does that to you repeatedly, you should consider the possibility that you're dealing with a sociopath.

When the person is one of your parents, this realization can be incredibly painful, but also freeing and life-changing. Typically the children of sociopaths desperately try to make sense of their parents' behavior. They can be very creative in trying to explain the unexplainable. Here are a few of the many excuses I've heard the adult children of sociopaths come up with to try to make sense of their parent's hurtful, underhanded or ruthless behaviors:

"He has anxiety"
"She doesn't really mean it"
"Something's wrong with her brain"
"He just cares too much"
"She can't help it"
"He had a difficult childhood"

To better understand what these adult children are trying to explain away, let's check in again with Zeke, right after he hands his sociopathic mother the note.

ZEKE

Zeke watches his mother read the note. As she does so, he sees her lips compress in a thin, hard line of displeasure.

"What?! How could you do this, Zeke? I'm so embarrassed that you would behave this way at school."

Zeke's eyes begin to brim with tears. "I" he starts to say.

His mother interrupts him. "Not a word from you. I don't want you to speak or even look at me. Go to your room right now and write, "I will never get in trouble at school again" 50 times, and it had better be in cursive. And it had better be readable. I don't want to see your face until you're done, and that means no dinner for you."

After spending four hours in his room, writing and crying and crying and writing, Zeke manages to write the sentence only 20 times, and none of them in cursive. He feels cold terror in his heart because he knows his mother will be enraged when she sees he printed. There's no help for this, however, because he's far from mastering cursive writing at his age, having only just been introduced to it at school. But he's hungry and sad and feels desperately guilty that he's angered his mother so. He draws a heart on the bottom of the paper for his mother, and gingerly ventures from his room to where his mom is watching TV. "Mom, I can only do 20. I promise I won't get in trouble again. Can I pleeeease stop?" he says meekly. Zeke's mother doesn't take her eyes off the TV so she doesn't see his mussed hair, exhaustion or tear-streaked face. "Get back in your room now," she growls. Or I'll give you something to really cry about. And for coming out of there before I said, you can write it ten extra times." She stands menacingly and starts walking toward Zeke. Zeke knows it's time to retreat. He runs to his room, falls on his bed and cries himself to sleep.

Notice that in this interaction Zeke's mother has exhibited an extreme lack of familiarity with her own child. She's unaware of what he can and can't do developmentally (whether or not he can write that much or in cursive) and of his feelings (empathy). She's also shown an extreme and unhealthy need to wield power over him (control). Also, she's shown cruelty and a willingness to hurt her son emotionally that borders on sadism (taking enjoyment in hurting others). While extreme and harsh punishments are a hallmark of sociopathy, not all sociopathic parents necessarily mete out extreme consequences. Some give no punishments and exercise their need to control in other ways, through the use of guilt or behind-the-scenes manipulation, for example. The common factor for all sociopathic parents is that to them, raising a child is much like everything else; it's all about power and control.

WALLACE

Forty-seven-year-old Wallace came to therapy after the death of his elderly father. Not because he wanted help with grief, but because of his extreme burden of guilt in his relationship with his mother. Wallace lives two hours away from his parents, yet for the last two decades he's visited them only once per year, or even less. When I explored this with him, it became clear that as long as he could remember, he's felt guilty about this. He told me that he felt like a most uncaring and unappreciative son for not visiting his parents enough. Yet he reported that almost every time he visits them, he gets either depressed or physically ill. "It makes me not want to go there. Also, my wife really hates to visit. Probably because my mom dislikes her."

Wallace described his recently deceased father as a workaholic who was not around much or very involved in his life. He described his mother as a "difficult person." When I asked Walter questions about this, he explained, "Nothing I can do has ever been enough for her. She resents my wife, and I think it's mostly because she feels that my wife took my attention away from her." Wallace explained that his mother feels that he is a selfish man for visiting so little, and she tells him so, directly or indirectly, every time they talk or see each other. Over the years she has expressed her disappointment in his lack of devotion to her via various means.

He told me one story which in a nutshell shows his mother's sociopathic style:

One Christmas Wallace and his wife and kids decided to bite the bullet and succumb to his mother's wishes. They hadn't visited his parents for almost a year, and knew that they needed to put in an appearance at the Christmas dinner his mother was putting together. Wallace's mother was delighted that he was coming, even making the sweet potato recipe that was his childhood favorite. The visit seemed to be going remarkably well until it was time to open gifts. As the grandchildren excitedly tore into the brightly wrapped packages to see what their grandparents had given them, Wallace's heart sank. He realized that his mother had again expressed her disappointment in his lack of attentiveness to her. This time she had made her point by giving her other grandchildren expensive new iPods, and Wallace's children cheap plastic toy cameras. Wallace's children expressed polite thanks to their grandparents. But Walter could tell that they were mystified and hurt by the dramatic gap between their gifts and the gifts that their cousins received.

Later that day when he had an opportunity to speak privately with his kids, Wallace tried to explain to them the

> inequality of the gifts. He told them that their grandparents were elderly and didn't realize how different the gifts were. But he felt that this was one incident that he couldn't let go. He knew that he had to confront his mother about it He found her alone in the kitchen and asked her if the gifts were a way of trying to tell him something. "Is Christmas to you only about how expensive the gifts are Wallace? You've never cared about anything but money. Next year I'll be sure to spend more on your children if that makes you happy." Then she added, "I guess that's what I should expect from someone too busy to visit his own parents."
>
> That evening at Christmas dinner Wallace's mother acted as though nothing negative had happened. She behaved as if Christmas was merry, as if everything was fine, and appeared to expect Wallace to do the same.

In this one story from his adult life, she has exhibited *all* of the traits of a sociopath. Trying to control him via underhanded means, viciously attacking him and then acting as if the attack hadn't happened, painting herself as the victim (neglected mother), and blaming Wallace (selfish son). In addition, she was willing to hurt her grandchildren in order to hurt her son.

As Wallace and I worked together over time he was able to see that the guilt he was taking on was misplaced. His mother (and, by not intervening, his father) had driven him away with these kinds of controlling, punishing behaviors throughout his childhood, adolescence and adulthood. He was getting depressed and sick during visits because he didn't understand what was happening. He was swallowing his mother's toxins because he had grown up with them and couldn't see them for what they were, partially blaming himself instead. Recognizing his mother as a sociopath helped him understand that he needed to protect himself and his children in whatever way was necessary. He was then freed up to focus on that instead of on his misplaced guilt.

If you have any question about whether your parent (or anyone else in your life) might be a sociopath, see the References at the end of this book for information about the book *The Sociopath Next Door*.

Type 11: Child as Parent

This type of parent actually allows, encourages or forces his child to behave as if he is a parent, not a child. Sometimes the child must parent himself, and sometimes he must parent his siblings too. In the most extreme examples a child can even be called upon to parent her own parent. In the large majority of these families there is some sort of extreme hardship which forces the child to suddenly become an adult. Some of the parenting types we've already talked about are good examples of families with such hardship. Take, for instance, the bereaved family, the family with an ill family member or the family in which there's an addicted or depressed parent. Another example might be a family with financial difficulties such that both parents are forced to work long hours. In all of these there's some reason why the real parent is not performing the parental functions so that the child has to step up and take them over.

ZEKE

Third-grader Zeke walks home with the note from his teacher in his pocket. He rushes along as fast as he can, because he knows that he has to get home before his five-year-old sister gets dropped off from kindergarten by the neighbor. She's too young to be home alone, and his mother won't be back from her job cashiering at the local Stop & Shop until 8:00p.m. Zeke doesn't give even a tiny bit of worry to his note. He knows that his mother won't be upset because she knows how responsible he is. She relies on him, and trusts him to take care of his sister, make them both peanut butter sandwiches for dinner and get his sister into her pajamas before she gets home from work. She won't yell or be worried.

Here Zeke's lack of concern about his mother's reaction shows that he doesn't see himself in the child role. He's essentially playing an adult role with all of his responsibilities with his little sister. Also, those responsibilities give him a status in which he has more power and authority than he should have with his mother. In the absence of a parent/child boundary, Zeke stands to learn nothing from the incident at school. Zeke is essentially missing out on childhood, which puts him at risk for more rebellious behavior as an adolescent. But unless his circumstances change, he'll very likely grow up to be an overly responsible adult who has difficulty knowing what he feels, what he wants, or that either matters. This is a set-up for the empty, disconnected feeling that many emotionally neglected adults experience.

That said, it's very important to take note of one key thing:

Being in a family that's compromised in some way–single parent, sick parent, sick sibling, or financial hardship, for example–is by no means a sentence for Emotional Neglect. Many, many parents who are coping with challenges such as these do manage to stay attuned to their child and provide him with the care and attention he will need in order to feel connected and "filled up" as an adult. In fact, spending a lot of time with your child is not even a requirement for preventing Emotional Neglect. You can be aware of your child's feelings, help him understand himself, and stay in tune with his emotional needs without spending tremendous amounts of time with him. Time helps make it easier, but a lack of it can be overcome.

To illustrate this important point, let's revisit Sally.

SALLY

Remember Sally, whom we talked about in the Type 4 Bereaved Parent? Sally's father died of cancer when she was young. This loss of her father had a profound effect on her personality and functioning as an adult. Remember that no one had told the children that their father was likely to die. Sally was told "Daddy's gone" by her sister, not by her mother. After Sally's father died, her mother seldom spoke of him again. The children were left home alone after that point to essentially care for and parent themselves because their mother had to work long hours in a menial job to support the family.

Which aspects of this scenario do you think led to Sally's feelings of emptiness and of living in a colorless world as an adult? The death of her father? Her mother's long hours after the death? The financial hardship that followed?

The answer is none of the above. All of those factors are things that *happened*. They're events. Events themselves don't cause Emotional Neglect. If Sally's mom, in the thick of her own grief, had had the ability to be emotionally attuned to the needs of her children, things could have turned out very differently.

The cause of Sally's Emotional Neglect was not the loss of her father. Nor was it what *happened* after her father's death. The cause was actually what *didn't happen* before and after her father's death. No communication from her parents about dad's illness. No emotional preparation of the children for what was to come (dad's protracted illness and death). No careful, gentle sharing of the news of the death. No attention from parents and other adult family members to the children's confusion, shock and grief after the death. No allowing the children to talk and share their feelings in remembrance of their dad, or to make sense of their feelings and give each other emotional support.

All of these factors are *the absence* of something. They're the white space in the family picture, the background rather than the foreground.

That's why Sally would have so much difficulty, as an adult, seeing what was wrong with her and why.

Type 12: The Well-Meaning-but-Neglected-Themselves Parent

Even the most loving and well-meaning parents can be emotionally neglectful. As noted at the beginning of this chapter, the WMBNT parent type probably makes up the largest subset of emotionally neglectful parents. After reading about all of these different types of emotionally neglectful parents, you're probably developing a sense of how a loving, caring parent can be emotionally neglectful. It is entirely possible for a parent who loves and wants the best for his child to emotionally neglect her. The truth is, to *love* your child is a very different thing from being *in tune* with your child. For healthy development, loving a child just isn't enough. For a parent to be in tune with his child, he must be a person who is aware of and understands emotions in general. He must be observant so that he can see what his child can and can't do as he develops. And he must be willing and able to put in the effort and energy required to truly know his child. A well-meaning parent who lacks in any one of these areas is at risk of emotionally failing his child.

To get a better idea of how WMBNT parenting works and repeats itself, let's revisit Zeke one last time.

ZEKE

Zeke walks home from school with the note from his teacher in his pocket. His Mother is in the living room watching Oprah. "Hi, Zeke, how was school?" she calls out from the other room. When he walks into the living room and nervously tries to hand her the note, she asks him to wait a minute until a commercial comes on. He stands for a moment with the note in his hand, and then retreats to his bedroom to play video games. He leaves the note on his bureau. The next day his mother finds the note when she goes

> *to put some laundry in his drawer. As she reads the note, she is*
> *momentarily bothered. But she thinks to herself, "Wow, Mrs.*
> *Rollo sure overreacts to things." and puts the note and the*
> *problem behind her.*

In this example, Zeke's mom, although a loving mother, is not attending to the *feeling* level of life. She didn't sense whatever Zeke might have been feeling about having to hand her a note from his teacher, such as anxiety or consternation. She does not see a reason to be concerned about his disrespect at school because she's blind to the connection between behavior, feelings, and relationships (in this case the relationship between Zeke and Mrs. Rollo). She places no value on Mrs. Rollo's feelings, considering them an "overreaction." These are sure signs of a person who is not aware or in touch with the world of emotion, and who lives mostly on the surface of life.

Many of the parents we've already talked about in this book could very possibly fall into this category in addition to their own type. Let's go back and take a look at all of the parents we've already discussed who may potentially be WMBNT.

- **Sophia**, **Joseph** and **Renee**'s Authoritarian parents. Many authoritarian parents were raised by such parents themselves. They love their children, but authoritarian parenting is all they know.
- **Samantha's** and **Eli's** Permissive parents had the misguided belief that it is loving to let their kids do as they wish.
- **Sally's** Grieving mother loved her children, and did the best she could to take care of them. She simply didn't have the emotional skills to be in touch with their feelings or help them manage them. It's likely that her parents didn't teach her those skills.
- **Margo's** Depressed parents clearly loved her. They may not have realized what was missing in their parenting of Margo because they didn't receive it from their own parents.

- **Sam's** Workaholic parents wanted to provide the best for him. They mistakenly thought material wealth would result in a happy, well-adjusted child.
- **Tim's** Achievement/Perfection-Focused parents had raised him this way, and he was in turn raising his children this way.

None of these well-meaning people probably had any idea that they were not providing their children with the fuel that they would need for a happy, connected life. They were each simply recreating what they had experienced in their own childhoods.

One of the unfortunate aspects of Emotional Neglect is that it's self-propagating. Emotionally neglected children grow up with a blind spot about emotions, their own as well as those of others. When they become parents themselves, they're unaware of the emotions of their own children, and they raise their children to have the same blind spot. And so on and so on and so on.

There will be more examples given in this book of Well-Meaning-But-Neglected-Themselves parents. See if you can identify them as you read Part II.

PART II

OUT OF FUEL

Chapter 3

THE NEGLECTED CHILD, ALL GROWN UP

T hink of childhood as the foundation of a house. Think of adulthood as the house. It is certainly possible to build a house with a flawed foundation, and in fact it may look exactly the same as a well-built house. But if the foundation is cracked, crooked or weak, it will not be an important source of strength and security. It's not a noticeable flaw, but it could place the structure of the house itself at risk: one strong wind, and it comes tumbling down.

Adults who grew up emotionally neglected often seem normal on the surface, but are frequently unaware of the structural flaw in their foundation. They also have no idea that their childhood played a role. Instead they tend to blame themselves for whatever difficulties they may be experiencing in life. *Why do other people seem happier than me? Why is it easier to give than to receive? Why do I not feel closer to my loved ones? What is missing within me?*

You will meet many people in these pages–typically very intelligent, likeable, and lovable folks, who have grappled with these questions. They are far better at giving than at receiving. They tend to guard the secret of their emptiness quite carefully, so it is very difficult for anyone to notice what's missing. Only the closest people in their lives get even the slightest glimpse.

Everyone's experience is different. There are 6 billion people in the world, and no two stories are the same. But when dealing with Emotional Neglect, I see certain common themes arising in the adults who grew up this way. In this chapter, we'll go through some of those themes. They are:

1. Feelings of Emptiness
2. Counter-dependence
3. Unrealistic Self-Appraisal
4. No Compassion for Self, Plenty for Others
5. Guilt and Shame; What is Wrong with Me?
6. Self-Directed Anger, Self-Blame
7. The Fatal Flaw (If People Really Know Me They Won't Like Me)
8. Difficulty Nurturing Self and Others
9. Poor Self-Discipline
10. Alexithymia: Poor Awareness and Understanding of Emotions

People's reasons for experiencing these feelings are unique to their lives, but the issues are not without their common ties. You'll hear the story of Laura, whose parents didn't respond when over the years more than one friend committed suicide, making her believe that she shouldn't respond, either. I'll also tell you about Josh, whose mother was so busy building her career that she didn't give him any feedback, positive or negative, on which to build his identity. At the end of each section, I'll list a few signs and signals to help you determine if you fit this category.

But before you read on, one caveat. As you read the signs and signals listed, you may find yourself thinking, "Gee, I don't know anyone who doesn't have some of these." And you'll be right about that. Every human being has some of these characteristics and challenges. Keep in mind that I am speaking to people who have a *significant struggle* with these problems, and who intuitively feel as they read this book that they are reading about themselves.

1. Feelings of Emptiness

Few people come to therapy because they feel empty inside. It's not a disorder in and of itself like anxiety or depression. Nor is it experienced by most people as a symptom that interferes with their lives. It's more a generic feeling of discomfort, a lack of being filled up that may come and go. Some people experience it physically, as an empty space in their belly or chest. Others experience it more as an emotional numbness. You may have a general sense that you're missing something that everybody else has, or that you're on the outside looking in. Something just isn't right, but it's hard to name. It makes you feel somehow set apart, disconnected, as if you're not enjoying life as you should.

I have found that most emotionally neglected people who come to therapy for anxiety, depression, or family-related problems, for example, eventually express these empty feelings in some way. Typically the emptiness is chronic, and has ebbed and flowed over the course of their lives. It may be difficult to imagine what would make a person feel this way. The answer lies in emotional responses from parents during childhood.

We'll take a look at several examples of the causes of these feelings, the ways they manifest themselves, and the processes that fix them. To begin, let's look at a general example of emptiness brought on by emotionally neglectful parents.

Simon

Simon was a handsome, fit 38-year-old when he first came to treatment. His presenting problem was an inability to have a relationship, despite interest from plenty of women. Simon wanted to find out what was wrong, what was getting in his way. By all appearances, he was a wonderful catch; successful as a stock analyst, he drove a Porsche and owned a beautiful condo in Boston. He loved to skydive, and as a hobby restored old Porsches and raced them. Was he too particular in choosing women? Did he have a fear of commitment? It took some time in our work together for the real Simon to come out of hiding.

Simon was the child of wealthy parents. He grew up in a huge house with a lot of acreage, most of it wooded. His parents traveled often, leaving him and his younger sister at home with a nanny. His sister was disabled, so she needed lots of care. When they were home from their travels, they focused the majority of their parenting energy upon her, leaving Simon to his own devices. Remembering Chapter 2, you might see that Simon's parents would fit best into a combination of two Parenting Types: Parent of an Ill Sibling, and Permissive.

Simon's parents were truly pathologically disconnected from him. He generally ran free, with no limits or rules. As a child, he spent lots of time alone in the woods. As an adolescent, he became very active in drinking and smoking pot. When he got a DUI, his father showed brief concern, but it didn't last.

Simon shared a memory of often hanging out alone for hours amongst the trees behind his house as a teen, feeling restless, not wanting to go home because there was nothing for him there. He would maybe smoke a joint, delaying his return until long after dark, wanting to put off as long as possible the terrible feelings that he experienced when he walked through that door. He had intense anger toward his parents, which he couldn't understand or make sense of, mixed with an overwhelming feeling of aloneness, and a desperate wish that he had a girlfriend, a constant companion to fill the vast void that was his life.

After receiving some attention and concern from his father after his DUI, Simon got back on track, graduated from college and earned his degree in economics. He moved to Los Angeles and worked for a huge firm for several years. He was very successful and made lots of money. He developed a relationship with a woman which went fine until she wanted to get married. At that point, he began to feel numb and empty, and tired of Los Angeles. He abruptly broke off the relationship, quit his job, and moved to Boston. In Boston, he easily re-established himself in a new job because he was well-educated, marketable and able to demand a good salary.

Once he had established his new life, however, he soon discovered those old feelings of restlessness coming back. Something wasn't right; he still wasn't happy. This is when he began to skydive and race Porsches. He was trying to fight off his emptiness with extreme sports. The shot of adrenaline he got each time he jumped out of a plane worked miracles, but only briefly. On his drive home from a jump, the old feelings would seep back, the numbness, the emptiness, and he would start to wish that his parachute hadn't opened. He would imagine himself dead, and what a relief that would be. In fact, he had been plagued with thoughts like this off and on for years.

Simon wanted to die not because he felt too much, but because he felt nothing. He was unable to have a relationship because he was empty, incapable of giving *or* receiving. He moved through the world in a restless search for meaning, discarding jobs, condos, cars and people when they failed to deliver. He wanted what everyone else seemed to find so easily, but which proved elusive to him, a connection with another human being.

In therapy, my work with Simon focused on feelings. When he told stories about his life, I would often interrupt and ask, "And how did you feel right in that moment?" Or, "How do you feel right now, as you talk about this?" At first, Simon was irritated by my questions. He experienced them as interruptions, irrelevant tangents taking us in the wrong direction, away from the point he was trying to make with the story.

Gradually, however, over about two years of therapy, his mind began to open up to the world of emotion. In attempting to answer my queries, he slowly became able to turn his attention inward, focus on his inner experience, and put names to his feelings. Interestingly, as Simon became a more feeling person, he began to experience sexual problems with the woman he was dating. As he became more able to connect with his girlfriend emotionally, he became less able to have sex with her. His impotence became a source of great distress for him. The second part of his treatment, then, was helping him recognize that he was literally raised to be a lone wolf. That he had cut off his emotional self so completely in relationships that the mere concept of mixing emotional closeness and sexual intimacy terrified and threatened him. Most of us know that sex for the sake of sex is easy. Sex in the service of emotional intimacy? Well, that's a little more daunting. For Simon, when sex started to have meaning and feelings attached, it was more than he could handle. His body handled this for him by shutting down his ability to have sex.

Much to Simon's credit, he persevered. He was eventually able, through hard work in therapy, to grow more comfortable within himself. Three girlfriends later, he found a woman with whom he felt safe enough, emotionally, to enjoy true intimacy.

You may be wondering about the connection between Simon's feelings of emptiness, his numbness, and his relationship problems. They are all side effects of one core issue: Emotional Neglect. Simon's formative years were spent alone and lonely, with very little feeling between his parents and himself. The emotional substance that allows a child to connect to his parents, people, and the world in general, was absent. Simon grew up in an emotional vacuum. He tried to "fill himself up" with peers, pot and parties. He sought out girlfriend after girlfriend, hoping they would fill him with meaning and connection. None of these strategies worked. In the end, it took therapy to make him look inward, not outward, for the answer. He had to learn about emotions, accept that he had emotions, and allow himself to feel them in order to experience the substance, the richness, and the meaning in life. Only then was he capable of a relationship that had substance, richness and meaning.

The fuel of life is feeling. If we're not filled up in childhood, we must fill ourselves as adults. Otherwise, we will find ourselves running on empty.

Simon is, of course, a fairly extreme example of emptiness. Many neglected people have it in a much milder form and are not so tortured by it. But I have found that emptiness at its mildest interferes with a person's ability to engage in and enjoy life. At its most severe, it can drive people to consider, or even act on, suicide.

Signs & Signals of Emptiness
- **at times, you feel physically empty inside**
- **you are emotionally numb**
- **you question the meaning or purpose of life**
- **you have suicidal thoughts that seem to come out of nowhere**
- **you are a thrill-seeker**
- **you feel mystifyingly different from other people**
- **you often feel like you're on the outside looking in**

If you feel that several of the above signs describe you, it's important to consider the possibility that you were emotionally neglected. But don't despair. Once you've figured out which aspects of Emotional Neglect apply to you, you can correct and combat its effects.

2. Counter-Dependence

Everyone knows what dependence is. Webster's Dictionary defines it as "determined or conditioned by another; relying on another for support." Conversely, independence can be described as "not determined or conditioned by another; not needing to rely on another for support." Not many people have heard the term "counter-dependence." It's not a term that is in common use, and not a concept that is familiar to many. In fact, it's used mostly by mental health professionals. It refers to the drive to need no one, or more specifically, the fear of being dependent. Counter-dependent people go to great lengths to avoid asking for help, to not appear, or feel, needy. They will make every effort not to rely on another person, even at their own great expense. Here is an example of how an emotionally neglected child grew up to be counter-dependent.

David

When David first came to see me for therapy, he was a successful forty-something businessman with a wife and three children. He had done very well financially, and his children were all young adults who would be leaving home soon. He came seeking help for longstanding depression. David initially said that his childhood was happy and free. But as he told his story, it became evident that he had been greatly affected by the absence of a key ingredient.

David grew up the youngest of seven children. He was a surprise, born nine years after his next youngest sibling. When David was born, his mother was 47 and his father 52. David's parents were good, hard-working people who meant well, and he always knew they loved him. But by the time David was born, they were tired of raising children, and David essentially raised himself. His parents did not ask to see his report cards (all A's), and he didn't show them. If he had a problem at school, he didn't tell his parents; he knew he must handle it himself. David had complete freedom to do anything he wished after school because his parents seldom asked him where he was. They knew he was a good kid, so they didn't worry. Even though David enjoyed this extensive freedom from rules and structure, he grew up feeling deep within himself that he was alone. The message he internalized from the freedom was "don't ask, don't tell." He understood from a very early age that his accomplishments were not to be shared, nor his failures, difficulties or needs. Even though he couldn't recall his parents ever actually *telling* him such a thing, he absorbed it into the very fiber of his being that this was life for him. It became a part of his identity.

As an adult, David presented as emotionally constricted and self-contained. Others frequently described him as aloof. His wife, after 15 years of marriage, was at the end of her rope. She felt that David was incapable of connecting with her emotionally. He told her he loved her often, but seldom showed her any emotion, positive or negative. She pointed out that he was a wonderful provider, but described their relationship as empty and meaningless. David described himself as feeling empty inside. He revealed that the one person in the world he actually felt emotional about was his teenage daughter, and that he sometimes *resented her for being important to him*. David was dogged by wishes to be dead, which he couldn't understand since he had such a great life. His constant fantasy was of running away to live alone on a deserted tropical island.

The ingredient that was missing from David's childhood was emotional connection. Emotions were treated as non-existent in his family. There was little interaction of any kind between David and his parents, no positives, but none of the important negatives, either. He didn't get to see joy in their eyes as they looked at his report card, or experience their anxiety when he came home from school long after dark. David's relationship with his parents could be summed up by one word: cordial.

The message David's parents unwittingly taught him, completely outside of his own and their awareness, was "don't have feelings, don't show feelings, don't need anything from anyone, ever." His fantasies about being dead or running off to a tropical island were the best ways he could imagine to accomplish that mandate. David was a good boy who learned his lesson well.

Signs and Signals of Counter-Dependence
- you've had feelings of depression but you don't know why
- you have inexplicable, longstanding wishes to run away or simply be dead
- you remember your childhood as lonely, even if it was happy
- others describe you as aloof
- loved ones complain that you are emotionally distant
- you prefer to do things yourself
- it's very hard to ask for help
- you're not comfortable in close relationships

If you relate to some of these signs, you may have been emotionally neglected. Keep reading.

3. Unrealistic Self-Appraisal

If you were asked to describe yourself, how would you answer? What adjectives would you use? What would be the balance of positive vs. negative words and phrases? Most importantly, how *accurate* would your description be? In the book *Self-Esteem*, by McKay and Fanning, one exercise asks the reader to take an inventory of his self-concept. The reader is asked to list his strengths and weaknesses in a number of different areas, such as physical appearance, personality, relationships, and mental functioning. McKay and Fanning point out that people with low self-esteem tend to view themselves in a negatively skewed manner. They exaggerate their weaknesses and downplay their strengths.

It's true that many of the emotionally neglected have low self-esteem. But just as often, emotionally neglected adults paint *inaccurate* pictures of themselves, not necessarily negative, but simply *off*.

We develop our self-concept over the course of childhood and adolescence. When we see pride on our parents' faces after a piano recital, it is validation that we played well, and it makes us want to get better. When a parent says after a Little League game, "That was some good fielding today. Let's work on your batting." it provides vital feedback to the child about his strengths and weaknesses. As children, we are like little computers, taking in feedback from the environment, storing it in memory, combining that feedback with other feedback, and developing a cohesive idea of our skills, talents, deficits and shortcomings. We take in this data from teachers, coaches, and peers. But the most important data with the strongest impact comes from our parents. When this process goes right, it results in a balanced, realistic self-appraisal which is the foundation of self-esteem. Such a self-appraisal is the springboard for many choices in life, such as what to strive for, what skills to develop, what colleges to apply to, what to major in, what type of mate to seek, what career to choose. It can be helpful in maintaining and preserving self-esteem. For example, a person who is not accepted into medical school can say to himself, "I'm not as good at science as I am at math. If I want to be a doctor, I'm going to have to work extra hard and keep trying." Another person without such a solid sense of himself might feel devastated and inadequate, and give up.

Josh

Josh came to me at the age of 46 at the urging of his girlfriend. He was a divorced father of two sons, ages 12 and 10. Josh had been in therapy for years, but felt it had not helped him. He felt stuck, both in treatment and in life. He also was privately plagued by a feeling of being a misfit. Josh described himself on numerous occasions as a "square peg in a round hole." He'd had this feeling since childhood. As I got to know Josh, I came to understand the reasons why.

Josh grew up in a small, affluent town in Connecticut. An only child, his father left his mother when Josh was two years old and was seldom seen after that. His mother never remarried. She was a dean at a local university. Josh initially described his mother as loving and doting. But when we scratched the surface on that, it became clear that her "doting" was actually of the material type. She spent freely on him, buying him anything he wanted. Actually, throughout Josh's childhood, she was highly focused on her career, working long hours. He described himself as a childhood loner and dreamer. After school, he wandered through the woods around their rural home with his dogs, which were truly his best friends. It was the dogs that entertained him every free hour, and prevented him from feeling alone. Instead of encouraging him to have friends over, his mother was thrilled that he entertained himself and didn't require much from her, not because she didn't care about him, but because it freed her up to put everything into her work.

In middle school, Josh started to have some problems being bullied at school. His bookishness earned him the moniker "Dweeb" and although he tried to deal with it in many ways, his efforts only earned him the added title of "Feeb." Rather than helping Josh deal with this, and going through all that pain with him, his mother solved the problem by yanking him out, abruptly transferring him to a local exclusive private school. It's no surprise that Josh was even more unhappy there. He had lost a lot of confidence from the bullying. The name "Dweeb Feeb" still echoed in his head.

Josh's mother switched him to different schools two more times when peer problems arose, teaching him how to escape difficult situations, but not how to face or cope with them. He therefore didn't have the opportunity to work anything through, stand up to bullies, or feel any sense of mastery or strength.

When it was time to apply to colleges, Josh's mother adamantly insisted that he apply to the college where she was employed. When he resisted, she angrily washed her hands of his college search and left him to his own devices. On his own, he did get himself accepted to a good college, but graduated with a degree in English *based solely on the fact that he liked to read.*

It is important to note here that throughout Josh's upbringing, his mother was not taking note of his strengths and weaknesses, such as his love of animals, his facility with the outdoors, or his tendency to isolate himself from other kids. She was not **feeling an emotional connection** to Josh. She was not **paying attention**, and seeing him as a unique and separate person, and she was not **responding competently** to his emotional need. He was not seeing himself reflected in his parent's eyes, and therefore didn't develop a sense of his own abilities and challenges or a realistic self-appraisal or identity. When it came time for Josh to go to college, he found himself without that springboard from which to make decisions such as a college and a major and a career.

Despite his Masters Degree in English, Josh was under-employed when I met him, currently working as a truck driver delivery man for a construction supply company. He had difficulty feeling comfortable with his coworkers, as he was truly outside of his element in this job. He also found the work to be extremely tiresome and boring. Josh had tried teaching high school English for two years after receiving his Masters in his late thirties. But he gave up teaching altogether when he found himself criticized by parents and a school administrator for not having enough control over the classroom.

One of Josh's primary presenting complaints was of being incapable of choosing and committing to a career. He had great difficulty figuring out what he was interested in, what he would be good at, or where he might fit in. It was evident that he had low self-esteem and a fragile, poorly developed identity.

On the surface, Josh's mother loved him, but she did not truly "see" her child. She made decisions about his education based not on who he was and what he needed, but on who *she* was, and what *she* needed. Josh had very little opportunity to perceive his true qualities through his parents' eyes.

As an adult, Josh's identity was out of balance. In the absence of attention and feedback from his parents, his identity was incompletely developed, derived only from his own observations of himself. He described himself as "a loner," "a dreamer," "able to make good grades," "directionless." His self-appraisal was painted with broad, childlike strokes. It was devoid of the complexity and nuance with which healthy adults are able to see themselves. His view of himself was heavily weighted in the negative direction. It did not provide him with a firm foundation from which to make decisions about a suitable career path. It did not help preserve his self-esteem when he received criticism in the one career he had chosen and pursued for himself, teaching. Instead, in the face of negative feedback, he folded quickly and gave up.

Signs and Signals of Unrealistic Self-Appraisal

- it's hard to identify your talents
- you sense that you may tend to over-emphasize your weaknesses
- it's hard to say what you like and dislike
- you're not sure what your interests are
- you give up quickly when things get challenging
- you chose the wrong career or changed several times
- you often feel like a "square peg in a round hole," a misfit
- you're unsure what your parents think (or thought) of you

4. No Compassion for Self, Plenty for Others

Compassion is one of the highest forms of human emotion. It is what links us together both interpersonally and as a society. Compassion often fuels our donations to charity; it motivates Good Samaritan behaviors and can help us heal from life's wounds. It is the cement of friendships, and helps us forgive those who wrong us. There are two types of compassion: the compassion we feel for others, and the compassion that we feel for ourselves. Emotionally neglected people have plenty of the former, but little of the latter. They are often very forgiving of others' foibles and flaws, at least on the surface. Others find them easy to talk to because they appear non-judgmental and accepting. However, they tend to be quite judgmental and perfectionist when it comes to themselves. They can get very angry with themselves for a weakness that they would easily tolerate in another.

Noelle

Noelle is a 38-year-old married mother of a small child. She has an excellent education, holding advanced degrees from two Ivy League universities. She had a fast-track business career prior to motherhood. By all accounts, an outside observer would consider her a success. When I started treating Noelle for an anxiety disorder, she had recently been laid off and was floundering. It was clear that although she had much going for her on the outside, she felt something quite different on the inside. In fact, Noelle had a constant tape running inside her head saying "What's wrong with you? You can't even park a car right." "Why do you have to be overweight?" "For someone so intelligent, you are a lousy mother," "You're such a klutz," and so forth. Any tiny error would bring on a litany of interior judgment–judgment that she'd *never* apply to a friend or any other human being. How did Noelle develop such a skewed compassion barometer? It is rooted in her Emotional Neglect.

Noelle is the only child of parents who divorced when she was six years old. Her father was an alcoholic who was physically abusive to her mother. Noelle recalls several loud, frightening arguments prior to their separation. Noelle's mother was a social worker. She loved her daughter very much. She recognized her daughter's intelligence and often expressed pride about it to Noelle and to others. Noelle grew up knowing that she was smart, had the confidence to apply to very reputable schools, and indeed ended up with an excellent career. So what went wrong?

Soon after the separation, Noelle's mother remarried a man who immediately moved in with them. Although Noelle's mother loved Noelle very much, she had a history of severe childhood trauma and abuse herself, and she regarded this as her time to heal and be herself, for the first time in her life. She launched fully into her new independence and relationship, and paid less and less attention to her young daughter. Meanwhile, Noelle was left to manage her own difficult emotions about her changing life circumstances, her mother's new marriage, and the loss of her father. Her mother's lack of compassion for Noelle's predicament became Noelle's lack of compassion for herself.

In the absence of parental involvement and interaction, Noelle became her own parent. She microwaved frozen chicken sandwiches every morning for breakfast. She came home every afternoon to an empty house, where she sat and watched TV alone.

Noelle knew that she was exceptionally bright, and she wrapped herself in her intelligence like a warm cocoon that nurtured her soul. She had, therefore, little tolerance for any errors she might make because it disrupted her only security. Errors made her feel stupid. She scolded herself for her mistakes, thinking that it would help her to make fewer of them. She demanded of herself an A in every subject, and was very disappointed in herself for her few B's. There was no adult present in her life to put her mistakes into context, to help her understand how they happened, or to show her compassion for her disappointments. So she did not learn to do these things for herself. Instead, her harsh internal parent took the simple approach, and taught her that she'd better do everything exactly right, or suffer the consequences. As a result, she became paralyzed by disappointment and anger at herself.

While Noelle was busy parenting herself, other children who were emotionally nurtured were learning how to forgive themselves. When they brought home a poor grade, their parents would try to discern the reasons for it, talk to them about how to correct it, and communicate to the child that everyone slips and falls sometimes. This is how healthy children learn to pick themselves up, forgive themselves, understand and learn from their mistakes, put those mistakes behind them, and move on. Part of my work with Noelle was helping her, as an adult, to learn how to do this for herself.

Signs and Signals of Inadequate Compassion for Self
- **others often seek you out to talk about their problems**
- **others often tell you that you're a good listener**
- **you have very little tolerance for your own mistakes**
- **there is a critical voice inside your head, pointing out your errors and flaws**
- **you're much harder on yourself than you are on others**
- **you often feel angry with yourself**

5. Guilt and Shame: What is Wrong with Me?

As you can see from the above vignette, adults who were emotionally neglected can be quite perfectionistic and hard on themselves. For many, it does not stop there. When children are given the message from their parents that their feelings are a burden, excessive, or simply *wrong*, they will often begin to feel guilty and ashamed for having them. They will then make efforts to hide their feelings from others, or even to not have them at all.

Since many emotionally neglected adults were in no way abused, they recall their childhoods as happy and carefree. They can't pinpoint any factor on which to blame their problems, so they're left blaming themselves. Often, they grew up with lots of freedom, as did David and Josh. Since they were responsible for themselves as kids, they feel responsible for their imperfections as grown-ups.

When a child's emotions are not acknowledged or validated by her parents, she can grow up to be unable to do so for herself. As an adult, she may have little tolerance for intense feelings or for any feelings at all. She might bury them, and tend to blame herself for being angry, sad, nervous, frustrated, or even happy. The natural human experience of simply having feelings becomes a source of secret shame. "What is wrong with me?" is a question she may often ask herself.

Between her "happy childhood" and inexplicable emotions, she is left with the assumption that something is seriously amiss.

Laura

When Laura was 14, she rushed home from school one day as fast as possible, desperate to talk to her mother. She had heard at school that her best friend Sally's 16-year-old brother Todd had killed himself the night before. Laura had a secret crush on Todd, who was kind to his little sister and her friend, often teasing them and driving them to soccer practice. Laura was crushed by a wave of shock, confusion, and grief, a swirl of emotions she had not felt before.

When Laura got home from school, she hurried immediately to her mother, who had already heard the news. Her mother gave her a hug and said, "I'm not surprised this happened. I think he was into drugs." That was the end of the discussion. The topic was never mentioned again. Laura's mother didn't ever ask her how she felt, so Laura didn't ask herself that question. Instead, she pushed her feelings down, and tried not to think about it. In the ensuing weeks (during which she attended the funeral with only her friends since her parents didn't go), she focused on her friends, school and soccer, but avoided Sally. Seeing Sally made Laura feel awful. Laura found herself breaking into tears "for no reason" and at odd times, like during math class or in the shower.

By the time she graduated from high school, two more of Laura's acquaintances, both from her school, had committed suicide. She handled these losses as she had the first, except she skipped the part about telling her mother. She dutifully attended the funerals with her friends, and did not acknowledge how disturbed, confused and shocked she felt to anyone, including herself.

Laura had difficulty concentrating in school, and frequently lost her temper at home. As a result, she struggled more with schoolwork. Her parents became frustrated with her and would often ask, "What's wrong with you?" But it was a rhetorical question. They did not really want to know. Laura began to see herself as weak, stupid and uncooperative. She, too, wondered what was wrong with her. This self-view stayed with her all the way to adulthood. Generally, Laura described feeling emotionally numb. This was because she had successfully managed to cut off her feelings so that they wouldn't bother her. But each time she had strong feelings of any kind, for any reason, she felt weak and ashamed. At age 32, she told me in a therapy session, "I had a wonderful, privileged childhood, yet I wish I were dead. I have no excuse for being so depressed. Something is seriously wrong with me."

For Laura, the very act of having a feeling felt shameful and wrong. By experiencing her feelings as a burden, her parents had inadvertently given her the message that she was not to have them, and that if she did, she was never to express them, even to herself. Laura's emotions were her secret shame.

Signs and Signals of Guilt and Shame
- **you sometimes feel depressed, sad, or angry, for no apparent reason**
- **you sometimes feel emotionally numb**
- **you have a feeling that something is wrong with you**
- **you feel that you are somehow different from other people**
- **you tend to push down feelings or avoid them**
- **you try to hide your feelings so others won't see them**
- **you tend to feel inferior to others**
- **you feel you have no excuse for not being happier in your life**

6. Self-Directed Anger, Self-Blame

It is difficult to feel deeply ashamed of something as innately human in oneself as emotions without getting angry with oneself for it. Shame, taken one step further, becomes self-directed anger. Let's continue with our story of Laura.

Laura

As a teen and throughout adulthood, Laura was plagued by self-destructive feelings and fantasies. In college, after her boyfriend broke up with her, she took an overdose and was briefly hospitalized. Later, and throughout her adult life, she would purchase a six-pack of beer and drink it alone in her apartment. The more she drank, the more she would start to feel. She would begin to cry, which would turn to weeping, which would turn into feeling disgusted with herself for crying. She would then become filled with intense self-hatred. She would then make some cuts on her abdomen, which she found strangely comforting, and that enabled her to fall asleep. The next day she felt better, as if she had been somehow cleansed.

Laura went through her daily life numbly, with her feelings completely cut off and therefore outside of her awareness. She did not actually *feel* her anger, sadness or grief. This protected her from constantly feeling weak and ashamed. But those feelings were stored inside of her like the lava under a volcano. The beer allowed her to let some of the lava shoot out, which felt both intensely shameful and cleansing.

For Laura, the overdose and the cutting were expressions of self-directed anger. Deep down, Laura hated herself. Not for any *real* failings or shortcomings or flaws, but for being sad and hurt, and for being unable to explain to herself why she was sad and hurt. In her mind, she was damaged goods, and she had no excuse for it.

Signs and Signals of Self-Directed Anger and Blame

- **you get angry at yourself easily and often**
- **you use alcohol or drugs as a release**

- **you often feel disgusted with yourself**
- **you have self-destructive episodes or tendencies**
- **you blame yourself for not being happier and more "normal"**

7. The Fatal Flaw (If People Really Know Me They Won't Like Me)

One characteristic that most emotionally neglected adults share is a secret and carefully guarded feeling of being different or flawed. As you saw above, Laura felt ashamed of having feelings, which made her feel weak and damaged. When a person feels deep within himself that something is wrong with him, his natural tendency is to try to make sense of that feeling, or explain it to himself. Each emotionally neglected person comes up with his own unique explanation for "what is wrong with me," based upon his own particular childhood and family circumstances. I once put eight emotionally neglected women into a therapy group together, hoping that they would help each other to see the elusive acts of omission by those who had raised them that had led to so many of their difficulties. Over the course of a year, they had put a name to the common characteristic that they felt bound them together as a group. They called it the Fatal Flaw.

The Fatal Flaw is not a real flaw. But it is a *real feeling*. It is the emotionally neglected adult's deep-seated, buried belief about herself, the thing that makes her feel different from everyone else, estranged from the world, or unacceptable to others. It's held close to the chest, hidden away at all costs. The Fatal Flaw is a capsule, which contains within it echoes of the child's attempt to understand, "What is wrong with me?"

Emotionally neglected people tend to feel that they must keep their true selves hidden away from others, because if they let people get too close to them, their flaw will be exposed. For one person, the flaw might be a belief that he is worthless. For Laura, it was the secret shame that she was weak. For Noelle, it was a belief that she was stupid. But each emotionally neglected person has his or her own. Here's the story of Carrie.

Carrie

Carrie grew up the youngest of three children. Her father was a diesel mechanic and her mother a stay-at-home mom. She had a brother who was six years older and a sister four years older. She described her high-school-educated parents as homebodies, meaning that they were in no way adventurous, curious, or interested in the world. They were good, simple people who wanted only to work hard and raise their children. They did not think about the world in any complex way, and they certainly didn't pay the least bit of mind to what they themselves, or any of their children, might feel.

Carrie's mother had the exact same rules for Carrie and her sister, even though they were four years apart in age. She dressed them alike, cut their hair alike; they had the same bedtime, the same amount of freedom, and were required to do most everything together. Carrie's older sister felt the terrible injustice of this and resented Carrie for intruding on every aspect of her life. Neither Carrie nor her sister was treated as, or felt like, a self-contained, individual human being. They were treated as if they were two parts of the same person. Carrie grew up baffled, wondering why her older sister hated her so and trying her hardest to get into her sister's good graces. No matter what she did, her sister despised her. Her simple, child analysis of the situation was, "I'm not likable."

When Carrie (who as an adult discovered that she has Attention Deficit Disorder and learning disabilities) began to struggle academically in middle school, her parents did not notice. When she brought home a report card full of C's and D's, her mother's reaction was, "Well, it's OK, all you can do is try your hardest." Carrie gleaned from this comment that not much was expected of her because she didn't have much to work with in terms of intelligence. In the absence of any more complex explanations or higher expectations, she had developed two important assumptions about herself: she was unlikeable and she was dumb.

When Carrie had typical middle school friendship problems, she applied the same type of simple cause/effect analysis. Her explanation for every such incident was, "When people get to know me, they don't like me." This became her explanation for every break-up with every boy she dated, and for every social glitch that she encountered in her life.

By the time I met Carrie she was in her mid-thirties. She had developed an avoidant style, in which she very rarely initiated any social interaction, anticipating rejection around every corner. Carrie made me work hard in therapy. She offered very little of herself spontaneously. She was highly skilled at chitchat, but it was like pulling teeth to get her to talk with any depth about herself and her life. By avoiding substance, she was making herself uninteresting to others.

Carrie felt friendless and alone, and it was because she wasn't offering enough meaningful connection to keep friendships or relationships going. She claimed to want marriage and children, but gave up on every romantic relationship as soon as the man had any kind of issue with her, assuming that he, like all the others, didn't like her now that he knew her. Deep inside, she harbored a secret knowledge that she shared with no one and tried her best to hide, but which ruled her life: "If people get to know me, they won't like me." It was her Fatal Flaw.

Signs and Signals of the Fatal Flaw
- **you fear getting close to people**
- **it's hard to open up to even your best friends**
- **you tend to expect rejection around every corner**
- **you avoid initiating friendships**
- **it can be hard for you to keep conversations going**
- **you feel that if people get too close to you, they won't like what they see**

8. Difficulty Nurturing Self and Others

Nurturance can best be described as a combination of love, care and help. Children who are not *emotionally* nurtured can grow up to have a great deal of difficulty providing emotional nurturance to others. Remember David, the youngest of seven children, ignored as a child and unable to connect as an adult? Let's talk a little more about him.

David

As mentioned before, David's parents were hard-working, decent people who meant well. They provided a lovely home for him, nice clothes, and plenty of food. All of his material needs were met. His mother was a housewife, almost always physically present. David grew up *knowing* that he was loved by his parents. But he did not grow up *feeling* that he was loved by his parents. Not because they purposely didn't love him, but because feelings of all kinds, positive or negative, were not exhibited or allowed in their household. David was well-nurtured physically, but he did not receive emotional nurturance.

As an adult in a therapy group, David almost cringed when anyone in the group showed intense feelings. He was a master at offering practical, rational advice to any member who was in pain, but he did so with an absence of emotion. His advice was well-intentioned, but was delivered without feeling. His style did not go unnoticed by other group members, who would often get defensive and have trouble accepting his advice.

Most of us know that personal advice of any kind is best received when it is accompanied by a *feeling* of caring. Members of the group appreciated David's practical advice, but not his cold presentation. David was not able to emotionally connect to the people in the group, for fear that they might emotionally connect to him. They might grow to need him. They might actually depend on him. David often expressed a grave discomfort with being needed or cared for. Remember how David felt about his daughter? He resented her *for making him care about her.*

Like compassion, *nurturance* is an emotional glue that binds us together as people. It is the gas that fills our emotional tanks. It is a requirement for healthy parenting, and in a good marriage it should be abundant and mutual between husband and wife. When we receive nurturance from our parents as children, we internalize it and it becomes a part of us. As adults, we are then able to provide nurturance to others when they need it, be it our parents, our friends, our spouse or our children. Children are like sponges, absorbing their parents' love, care and help. A sponge too long away from water will go dry, and eventually harden. So too, a child too long away from love, care and help will harden and wall off, and will have trouble receiving and giving nurturance. This is what happened to David. He could neither feel nor express love.

Signs and Signals of Difficulty Nurturing Self and Others

- **people sometimes tell you that you come across as distant, or maybe even cold**
- **people sometimes think you're arrogant**
- **you often think others are too emotional**
- **others come to you for practical advice, but not for emotional support**
- **you feel uncomfortable when someone cries in your presence**
- **you are uncomfortable crying yourself, especially in the presence of another person**
- **you don't like the feeling that someone really needs you**
- **you don't like feeling needy**

9. Poor Self-Discipline

All of us need to use self-discipline every day and in many ways. We get up on time, shower, eat well, exercise, concentrate, do chores, save money. We learned how to make ourselves do these necessary tasks through the structure, love and expectations of those who raised us.

It is remarkable the number of emotionally neglected people who have tremendous difficulty with these things that we call self-discipline. I have found that the emotionally neglected often struggle to stop themselves from doing things they shouldn't, like eating junk food, over-spending, and other self-indulgences. Conversely, they also have difficulty forcing themselves to do things they don't want to do, like chores, tasks, work or exercise. Often they will say, "I'm so frustrated with myself. I just can't seem to get started." Yes, all of us struggle with this to some extent. But the emotionally neglected person's struggle is more chronic and intense. It becomes a lifelong theme. Emotionally neglected people will come to treatment calling themselves scattered, lazy, unmotivated, or procrastinators. When they talk about their childhood, you discover that their parents, however giving and loving, did not provide real structure for learning the skill of self-discipline. For example, they did not make the child do such things as his homework before he could go outside, chores and tasks around the house, or exercise to earn TV time.

Each time that a parent sets and enforces such rules and expectations, those rules and expectations become a part of the child's repertoire. The child learns a lesson in how to force himself to do something tedious. On the other hand, emotionally neglectful parents often do not stop the child from eating too much junk food, or from blowing all their money. When a child is left to his own devices, he will learn how to indulge himself. Emotional Neglect often sets us up for problems with self-indulgence.

Many emotionally neglected children have parents who love them very much and provide them with every physical need. But part of parenting is seeing your child for who he is: not only noticing the things that he's good at, but also noticing the things that are hardest for him, and putting in the effort to make sure that he addresses those. Many emotionally neglectful parents are very caring, but simply *are not involved with their child at that level.*

William

William came to therapy in his late thirties. He was dogged by a feeling that he should be achieving more. He had an MBA from a very reputable business school, and psychological testing that was done in his twenties had revealed that he had a very high IQ. Yet William had had a series of unchallenging jobs that did not use his degree or pay at the level that he should have been able to command. He recently had been laid off, and was concerned that his boss had not been totally happy with his performance.

William reported that he struggled greatly with self-discipline in both his professional and private life. At times he stayed up all night working and then overslept the next morning. His wife complained that he would sometimes forget to eat and rarely exercised. Despite his best intentions and efforts, he was very slow to start difficult, boring or unpleasant tasks. Once he did start such a task, he would immediately think of something better to do, and switch over to that. He had received feedback from employers that he was too slow in completing his work. He reported feeling very frustrated with himself for low productivity, stating, "I'm a terrible procrastinator," "I'm lazy," and "What is wrong with me?"

William's parents divorced soon after he was born, and his father was not a part of his life. As a single parent, his mother lavished love on him. He was the apple of her eye. And indeed William was a great kid. He was smart, popular, and didn't get into trouble. His teachers liked him, and his grades were good. His mother told him often that he was wonderful, and generally left him to do things on his own. She had to work a full-time job to support them, and she trusted that he would be fine without a lot of supervision from her. So William grew up with lots of freedom, lots of love, not much supervision and very little structure. He remembers doing term papers at the last minute, taking tests without studying, and running with friends all day and late into the night through middle and high school. He didn't have many chores or home responsibilities, and the ones he did have were very flexible. His mother was quick to relax the rules or let him off the hook. Likewise, if he had an academic slip his teachers would usually give him the benefit of the doubt because he was a bright, respectful kid with good intentions. Working outside his comfort zone and sticking with tedious chores were challenges that he seldom faced.

You're probably thinking that this sounds like a fun childhood. And yes, it was in many ways. But the problem was that it did not prepare William for the demands of adulthood. In his most recent job, he was required to work with clients to complete projects for them. He had to find out what the client wanted, lay out the plans for creating it, and deliver it by a deadline. In many of these projects he had to coordinate contributions from members of his team to make sure it all worked together. William loved this job and the creativity that it required of him. However, the coordination and scheduling aspects bored him to tears. When he had to do the final write-up, he would procrastinate. He missed deadlines, and his boss quickly became frustrated. This was a familiar pattern for William, and he grew insecure. William was smart enough, personable enough, and he needed and enjoyed the job. So what was missing?

The lack of struggle in William's childhood had prepared him very well for life as long as no unpleasant demands arose. As an adult, William is skilled at running free, metaphorically speaking. But when a boss demands results or he himself needs to strive for a goal, he does not have the self-discipline to make it happen.

As his mother took the path of least resistance by giving in easily and not pushing or structuring, so did William. William would have benefited greatly from regular kitchen duty at home, for example. If his mother had noticed his lack of challenge in high school, perhaps an advanced math or language class could have been found for him. More rules and structure at home would have helped William internalize rules and structure for himself. And conflicts with his mother about whether he wiped the counters properly might have taught him the importance of being thorough, even when doing a mundane, thankless task. William missed out on learning how to structure himself, or how to make himself do things he didn't want to do. Because he was a smart and personable kid, his lack of self-regulation went undetected until he entered the adult world of work. At which point it became clear that he ran short on an ability to tolerate boredom, an ability to structure himself, and an ability to persevere, all of which are necessary parts of every successful adult.

Signs and Signals of Poor Self-Discipline
- **you feel that you are lazy**
- **you're a procrastinator**
- **you have great difficulty with deadlines**
- **you tend to overeat, drink too much, oversleep or overspend**
- **you are bored with the tedium of life**
- **you tend to avoid mundane tasks**

- **you get angry at yourself for how little you get done**
- **you're an underachiever**
- **you have poor self-discipline**
- **you're often disorganized, even though you know you have the capacity to do better**

10. Alexithymia:

If there is one symptom that could be considered the common denominator of emotional neglect, it is probably alexithymia. It is present to one degree or another in every single emotionally neglected adult. The word "alexithymia" cannot be found in most dictionaries. It's not a word used by the general public. It's a word used primarily by psychologists and other mental health professionals, and mostly in research settings.

Alexithymia denotes a person's deficiency in, knowledge about, and awareness of, emotion. In its extreme form, the alexithymic is a person for whom feelings are indecipherable; both their own and other people's. The alexithymic lives his life with no willingness or ability to tolerate, or even experience, emotions. I have observed that many people with alexithymia have a tendency to be irritable. They tend to snap at others for seemingly no reason, and it obviously interferes with their relationships. It allows them to hold others at a distance, even as it leaves them feeling terribly alone.

Emotions that are not acknowledged or expressed tend to jumble together and emerge as anger. Eventually, suppressed feelings refuse to stay down. When they do, they erupt as small spurts of irritability that hurt others. Here is an example of an emotionally neglected man who was severely alexithymic.

Cal

Cal, a tall, thin man who looked almost emaciated, came for therapy in his mid-fifties. He was referred by his primary care physician in 1999 after he told her that he planned to kill himself at the end of the Millennium. In his first session, he was very clear about this plan. His angry and dismissive demeanor in our first session was striking. These hostile emotions were the only ones he was willing or able to display. As I got to know Cal, it soon became clear that he was both an alcoholic and an underachiever. Although he had a degree in engineering, he worked as an appliance repairman by day and drank beer alone in his apartment by night. He had never married, had no children, and lived alone.

For many years, Cal had fantasized about disappearing. After months of therapy, he was able to share this secret fantasy: he would run away to a bucolic forest and live as a hermit, without telling family, friends or anyone who knew him. He derived intense pleasure from imagining the reactions of sadness and shock of all who knew him when they heard he had disappeared, how worried and upset they might be, how they would wish for him to come back.

Cal had two older brothers and his parents were still living. In therapy, he expressed intense resentment, bordering on hatred, toward his entire family. He was unable to explain why he felt this way. But he reported that about one year prior to coming to treatment, he had dug out and destroyed every family picture he owned, including the ones of himself as a child. He was unable to give any explanation for this action, and did not respond to my curiosity about it with any curiosity of his own. Cal also had been put on probation several times at his work for snapping irritably at coworkers and customers.

As Cal talked in therapy, this all began to make sense. He grew up in a blue-collar town in upstate New York. His parents were second-generation German immigrants. His father worked in a factory and his mother stayed home to raise Cal and his two older brothers. There was no abuse in his family. Cal was well-protected, well-fed and well-clothed. When asked about his relationships with his brothers, he stated simply that he'd enjoyed playing baseball with his brothers until they hit middle school age, at which point they stopped playing with him. In fact, this was the only example he could give of any interaction of importance that had ever occurred in his family at all. When asked, Cal reported that in his memory, no one in his family had ever yelled, cried, hugged, kissed, touched, winked, or expressed emotion of any kind. In fact, Cal was quite perplexed by my questions about emotions. It was clear that he didn't speak the language of emotion. The concept of feeling was simply not on his radar screen.

However, anger was the one emotion that *was* familiar to Cal. He felt it very often, essentially all day every day. He tried to control it at work (so he wouldn't get in trouble with his boss), and he drank it away at night so that he could fall asleep. Despite its omnipresence in his life, he was not aware that he had it. He didn't notice it; he didn't question it. He was, however, comfortable with it because it was a part of him, like an arm or a heartbeat.

The nature of his Emotional Neglect had left him severely emotionally stunted. In all of his relationships–unable to understand what he felt or to read what others felt, unable to know what he could ask of someone or what he had to offer them–he was emotionally crippled and alone. No wonder he drank. No wonder he fantasized about leaving others behind to miss him and regret that they hadn't been there for him. And small wonder that thoughts of suicide soothed him when indecipherable emotions leaked from the lockbox that was his life history. After all, it is only emotion and connection which bring meaning to this strange thing we call existence.

The first stage of therapy for Cal was to become aware of his anger. The second, more difficult stage was to help Cal stop drinking as a way of stuffing his emotions, and to teach him to sit with his emotions. The third and most difficult stage was to help Cal pry open the lockbox called anger and to label and experience all the emotions that were stored within it.

As Cal formed a trusting relationship in therapy, he was able to see that when his brothers stopped playing baseball with him, it was more than just an incident. At that time, and still, Cal felt abandoned, hurt, excluded, unloved, unimportant. He had not identified, acknowledged or named those feelings. He had instead internalized them, adding them to the lockbox.

As a tribute to Cal, and at the risk of making the reader feel sad, I would like here to complete his story. As Cal learned to recognize and name his feelings, he visibly softened. Over several years of therapy, he became more open to his friends, who responded by calling him more. As his therapist, I began to hear about old acquaintances who were emerging from the woodwork, and were calling and spending time with him. He stopped drinking, and started teaching himself how to cook. Instead of drinking alone at night, he was sometimes out with friends and sometimes home making a big pot of chili or a pot roast. He gained weight and appeared physically stronger and healthier. His plan for suicide was gone.

Cal was able to enjoy his newfound connection to the world only briefly. He had been sober for two years when a spot was discovered on his lung. The cancer traveled to his brain and he was given nine months to live. During those nine months, he continued to come to therapy as long as he was physically able. His friends took turns sitting with him, visiting him in the hospital and cooking for him. At the very end, he did not die alone, but in the company of friends. His primary care doctor called me to tell me of his death. We cried on the phone together because we both had grown to love him.

Cal left me with an invaluable lesson learned, a parting gift: the scars of Emotional Neglect do not have to be permanent. And it is never too late.

Signs and Signals of Alexithymia

- **you have a tendency to be irritable**
- **you are seldom aware of having a feeling**
- **you are often mystified by others' behavior**
- **you are often mystified by your own behavior**
- **when you do get angry, it tends to be excessive or explosive**
- **sometimes your behavior can seem rash to yourself and others**
- **you feel that you are fundamentally different from other people**

- **something is missing inside of you**
- **your friendships lack depth and substance**

Henry David Thoreau said, "The mass of men lead lives of quiet desperation." I am convinced that he was referring to the legions of people who are wounded in childhood, without being able to recognize, label, or grow beyond it. It is my sincere hope that this book will allow you to see the remnants of this within your own life, and to summon the courage to conquer your own Emotional Neglect.

Chapter 4

COGNITIVE SECRETS: THE SPECIAL PROBLEM OF SUICIDAL FEELINGS

This chapter will talk about a subject that no one likes to talk about, and most people don't even want to think about. If you have never considered suicide and don't know anyone who has, feel free to skip this chapter. I promise it will not take away from your overall experience of reading this book, and you will not get anything less out of it.

If you have ever been affected in any way by suicidal thoughts or actions of yourself or another person, then read on.

The subject of suicide is both unpleasant and scary. For most of us, it's unimaginable, unthinkable. Some people think of suicide as a selfish act. Others see it as an act of cowardice. Most of us spend our lives doing everything in our power to avoid death. It is very difficult to grasp what must motivate a person to bring death upon himself. It must require something very dramatic such as a serious negative *event*, right?

Even though we tend to do everything in our power to avoid this subject, many people know someone who has considered, attempted or committed suicide. According to the National Institute of Mental health, in 2007 there were 34,598 suicides in the United States. That's 95 suicides per day. Suicide was the seventh leading cause of death for males and the fifteenth leading cause of death for females in 2007. These statistics do not include the 1,045 suicide attempts that occur every day in the U.S. And they certainly do not include the untold numbers of people who quietly contemplate killing themselves over long periods of their lives.

People kill themselves for an infinite number of different reasons. Sometimes it really is something very dramatic, as noted above; a response to an extreme negative event, like a public failure or humiliation. Other times it's a person's attempt to avoid the consequences of his actions; a prison sentence, for example. Still others kill themselves due to bipolar disorder or severe or chronic depression. Although always shocking and baffling to the community and to the loved ones left behind, it's at least possible to have some clarity about *why* when there is some clear event or disease that can be identified as the catalyst. This is, however, not always the case.

ROBYN

32-year-old Robyn lives in the heart of Seattle. She has a natural, downplayed attractiveness which makes people notice her. She has long auburn hair which she usually wears caught up in a barrette or a haphazard ponytail. When people first meet Robyn, they can't help noticing the unusual combination of auburn hair and crystal blue eyes, and Robyn receives many comments on it. Most people feel they're complimenting Robyn when they mention it, and are surprised when she looks embarrassed in response. Actually, Robyn is very uncomfortable with the fact that her appearance is noteworthy or unusual. Even at age 32, she tries to downplay her looks, as she is much more comfortable when she's able to keep herself in the background.

Robyn is single, never married. She earned a B.S. in psychology at age 21, but after a couple of years working at various jobs, she decided that it wasn't possible to make a living with it. At that point she went back to school and now has an M.B.A from UCLA. She has a great job which pays well and a nice condo in a lovely downtown neighborhood. She lives about a mile from her gym, and can often be seen running to and from the gym on weekends, taking care to get the right combination of aerobic and resistance training. Robyn's friends love to tease her about her healthy habits. She's a careful eater and has a phobia of eating grilled food, as she read somewhere that charred foods can cause stomach cancer. Friends good-naturedly have canned tuna on hand when they invite Robyn to a cook-out. Any extra trouble is made up for by the fun they have teasing her about her eccentric pet peeve, which Robyn takes well.

Robyn's friends describe her as a contradiction. They feel they can tell her anything because she's great at listening and giving advice, and can be counted on for solid, thoughtful feedback. But she seldom shares much about herself. She's good at giving, but she doesn't ask her friends for support or advice. On top of that, she can at times be impossible to track down. She can go weeks at a time not answering her phone. Her friends joke that "Robyn's in hermit mode." While she will accept invitations to social activities, she seldom initiates any. In fact, the majority of Robyn's friends have never seen her condo. Her general demeanor is quiet and in the background, but if she has a few drinks, she is the life of the party. Her wry sense of humor emerges, and she becomes hilarious and even socially daring. Friends sense a depth in her, but sometimes feel frustrated that they cannot reach it. It's as if Robyn is an excellent friend, but when she's in "hermit mode," she is completely inaccessible.

One Saturday night in June, Robyn went to her friend Trish's house for a cookout. Trish had a new recipe for lemon martinis, and they were surprisingly delicious. While everyone else had grilled steak tips, Robyn had her requisite tuna sandwich, and 3 lemon martinis. As usual, she was ridiculously fun that night. They played poker until the wee hours of the morning, and finally decided they were done in for the night and went home.

Two days later, Trish received a phone call from Robyn's sister with shocking news. Robyn had been found unconscious by her sister, who dropped by to visit and was alarmed that Robyn didn't answer the door. Robyn had taken an overdose of pills on Sunday, the day after the cookout.

No one in Robyn's circle of friends, family or coworkers could make sense of her self-destructive action. How could such a smart, successful, loved person do this? She had everything to live for. Why would she try to take her own life? Why were there no signs? Why didn't somebody pick up on some indication that Robyn might be planning to kill herself? All of Robyn's loved ones racked their brains trying to come up with a clue that they had missed. They found themselves analyzing every second of every minute of every moment they had spent with Robyn in the prior week. No one, including her friends at the cookout, could come up with a single thing.

There are many, many suicides which seem unattributable to any event or illness. These are sometimes folks who appear to be at the top of their game: Harvard students, successful business people, high school athletes who are making straight A's. Or it may simply be a friend, neighbor, colleague or sibling whom everyone thought was fine. Sometimes there is an identifiable trigger, but it does not seem significant enough to lead someone to kill him or herself. Often the person's loved ones are left not only in shock, but also mystified and confused. Those left behind end up grappling with unanswerable questions, not only *how could they do this*, but *why did they do it?*

To try to answer this question, let's now go back to Robyn. So far, you have experienced her the same way that her friends and family have. From the outside. Now we will go to Robyn's interior world, to understand, from the inside out, why she would take such an extreme action, and what really has been going on for her.

ROBYN

Robyn grew up in a small, peaceful town in Washington state. She was the third of five children of loving and attentive parents. Her father worked as a mechanical engineer, and her mother stayed home with the children until they all entered their teens, at which point she went back to work, as a teacher's aide in their local school system.

In many ways Robyn's childhood was fine. She and her siblings were all close in age. They lived in a tree-lined neighborhood loaded with families and children, so Robyn was never lacking for a playmate. She was close with her sisters. Her family, while by no means wealthy, had plenty of money for a good life, so there was no financial stress, and they never had to go without. Every April they packed up and flew to Disney World for a week, and every December they spent the week of Christmas and New Year's in Portland, Oregon with Robyn's grandparents.

Robyn's parents seldom argued, and they had very low tolerance for negativity of any kind. When a conflict would break out between the children, as they do with all siblings, the parents would crack down by sending all parties to their rooms immediately. It didn't matter what the fight was about, or if one person was clearly in the right or being victimized. The parents' motto was "Zero Tolerance." They also applied this rule to complaining, or any expression of unhappiness, sadness or frustration. The result was a quiet household. The children learned early on that if they had something negative on their minds, they had better keep it to themselves. Mom and Dad refused to be burdened by such nonsense. They wanted this to be a happy, cooperative household where everyone got along and no one was dissatisfied. Also, with five children to manage, they felt they didn't have the time and energy to put into solving crises, assuaging tears and soothing frustrations. The Zero Tolerance policy allowed them to stay in charge of the household, and, they felt, keep a positive outlook on life.

Robyn and her siblings were seldom in the house. From an early age, they far preferred running free in their neighborhood with their siblings and friends. Outside of the house, they were free to complain, fight, and express their thoughts and feelings, both positive and negative. Robyn's siblings found this refreshing and freeing. They were able to figure out that the feelings that their parents wouldn't tolerate were acceptable elsewhere. However, Robyn was different.

Robyn had been a sensitive child from birth. Her parents' third baby, they noticed right away how her personality differed from her older siblings. She cried a lot. She fussed when her mother put socks on her or gave her a new, unfamiliar pacifier. Her parents nicknamed her "Frequent Crier," a jokey take on the phrase "Frequent Flyer." As she grew into toddlerhood and eventually kindergarten and school age, she received plenty of good-natured ribbing from her family members because she was so quick to tear up. Quiet tears tended to lead to silly ribbing. But vocal crying was another matter. If Robyn's tears made noise, her parents enacted Zero Tolerance policy, and she was immediately sent to her room.

Throughout all of this, Robyn learned a powerful lesson. She learned that negative emotion was bad and would not be tolerated. She learned that any feelings she had that were not upbeat, fun or positive must be kept to herself and carefully hidden. She felt ashamed that she had such feelings, and silently vowed to never let them be seen. Over time she learned this lesson so well that she hid her negative emotion even from herself. She made sure to keep herself positive and upbeat at all times. When periodically she reached a point where she was unable to appear upbeat, she withdrew completely, holing herself up in her condo. She would then spend all of her time either at work, absorbed completely in her job duties, or locked in her condo voraciously watching television shows. This helped her keep all thoughts and feelings at bay until she could regain her energy to continue fighting off all negativity and be "happy" again.

Robyn didn't just fight this battle. She lived it. Her life was organized around making sure that she did not reveal, see, know or feel anything negative from within herself. It took a tremendous amount of energy. She was so bent on hiding the shameful, negative part of herself (Robyn's version of the Fatal Flaw) from the world that she couldn't let anyone get to know her too well. This is why her friends were not invited to her condo. She was afraid that they might catch a glimpse of some part of her that she didn't want to be seen.

It's important to note that throughout all of this, Robyn was intensely lonely. She knew that her parents, family and friends loved her. But she didn't feel loved. It's hard to feel loved by people who don't really know you, and nobody really knew Robyn. Not even Robyn. She felt completely isolated from the rest of humankind. Other people seemed happy and complete. They seemed to know each other, to care for each other, and to be free. Other people didn't seem to hide parts of themselves or to have this struggle. Robyn felt that she was on the outside of life looking in, watching herself as if she were on a movie screen, disconnected, alone and utterly unknown. She often wondered about the point of being alive. If life is so empty, with so much suffering, pain and lack of reward, why live it?

Since adolescence, Robyn had had this "outside looking in" feeling. At age 13, she had started wondering what was wrong with her. She'd had a great childhood, so there was no explanation for how flawed she felt. There was something missing, something sick inside of her, a secret void. The only way she could soothe herself was to imagine being dead. Being dead would be such a relief. She did not have any intention to kill herself, but she reserved the possibility as a safety net. If she ever reached a point where she could no longer tolerate the pain, she could always end her life. Then there would be no more struggle, no more emptiness, no more loneliness, no more pain. Robyn used fantasies of being dead and her secret knowledge of her safety net as her chief method of soothing herself from age 13 all the way through her adulthood, but she had not breathed a word of it to a single soul.

Now let's go back to the day after the barbecue, when Robyn acted on her safety net. Here's what happened that day:

Robyn woke up with a moderate hangover and with memories of the excellent fun she'd had the night before. She poured herself some cereal and sat down in front of the TV. She felt a dark cloud hanging over her head, as she had been fighting off "hermit mode" for a couple of weeks. She felt exhausted, lethargic and empty, but above all, numb. She tried to make the numbness and emptiness go away by watching an old Andy Griffith episode. It didn't work, so she lay down on her sofa and started to imagine being dead, since that usually helped. This time, it didn't seem to work, and instead the emptiness and pain just got more intense. She stood up and paced from one end of her living room to the other, back and forth, back and forth. As she did so, the dark cloud got darker, the emptiness deeper. Some part of her preoccupied mind noted that The Waltons had come on after Andy Griffith on the TV. This made her flash back to a memory from childhood in which her family chided her relentlessly for crying over a Waltons episode. She suddenly felt intense shame and self-hatred pile on top of her emptiness. Desperate to stop the worsening pain, Robyn impulsively ran to her bathroom and swallowed every pill she could find in her medicine cabinet, many of which she had stored up just in case she ever got this desperate.

As you can see, the Robyn that everyone else knew and loved was not the real Robyn. She was essentially a time bomb, set to explode periodically. What was different about this particular situation that caused Robyn to act on her fantasy? It was not a dramatic event. It was a TV show that brought her shame and self-blame into full force at the worst possible moment. Robyn was already at risk before the The Waltons show came on. But the family memory of criticism and humiliation was the final straw, plunging her even deeper into her own well of impossible aloneness and isolation. Ultimately, all it took was a Waltons re-run.

Robyn was lucky that her sister stopped by. Many people like Robyn are not found until it's too late. These are the people who don't get help. They don't get to share or understand their pain, and they don't get to explain their final moments to anyone. These are often, I think, the people who leave their loved ones baffled and confused, never to understand what happened.

Now let's revisit some of the people we met in Chapter 3, who will help us look at this issue from some different angles. But first, let's pause to consider the possible relationship between suicidal feelings and Emotional Neglect. Here I would like to remind you that human beings are designed to feel emotion. When that design is short-circuited, first by emotionally neglectful parents and later continued by the child himself as an adult, it throws off the whole system. Imagine ice-cream made without sugar, or a computer program in which some of the most basic commands have been removed. Such is the malfunction of the human psyche when emotions are pushed out of it.

In many ways, emptiness or numbness is worse than pain. Many people have told me that they would far prefer feeling *anything* to *nothing*. It is very difficult to acknowledge, make sense of, or put into words something that is *absent*. If you do succeed in putting emptiness into words to try to explain it to another person, it's very difficult for others to understand it. Emptiness seems like *nothing* to most people. And nothing is nothing, neither bad nor good. But in the case of a human being's internal functioning, nothing is definitely something. Emptiness is actually a feeling in and of itself. And I have discovered that it is a feeling that can be very intense and powerful. In fact, it has the power to drive people to do extreme things to escape it.

Remember **Simon**, the handsome, successful 38-year-old who took up skydiving? You may recall that Simon had suicidal feelings because he felt so empty and numb. For him, life was devoid of connection, meaning and passion. The thrills of skydiving were short-lived, and were insufficient to give him a reason to want to live.

David, on the other hand, had internalized the message "Don't have feelings, don't show feelings, don't need anything from anyone, ever." His suicidal feelings were based upon his wish to fulfill this mandate which he had unwittingly absorbed from his parents. Since David was indeed a living, breathing human being with both feelings and needs, the only way he knew to accomplish that mandate was to be dead. Indeed, by the time I met him he had already essentially stopped engaging in life.

You may recall that **Laura** went through her life with her feelings completely cut off. She used beer and cutting to release them, but paid for it with intense shame. Laura lived in a prison of her own self-perceived flaws. She felt like damaged goods, unlovable and disconnected. Laura's suicidal feelings stemmed from her anger at herself for having feelings and needs that she was unable to accept, acknowledge or abolish. In these ways, she was similar to **Robyn.**

Cal had a plan to kill himself at the end of the millennium. The idea of dying in a big way was comforting to him, because he felt that people around him would finally be able to see the pain that he had been forever unable to communicate to them through words. When Cal was overcome by emotion, he used this grandiose escape fantasy to soothe himself.

I believe these four emotionally neglected people were at high risk of acting upon their suicidal feelings. If they had not entered treatment in time, they each had the capacity for genuine self-harm. Here are some factors that all four plus Robyn had in common:

- emptiness and numbness
- suffering in silence
- questioning the meaning and value of his or her life. (what's the point of living?)
- escape fantasy

It's important to note that David, Laura, Robyn and Cal all had loving, well-meaning parents. They all grew up in comfortable middle-class homes and were well cared for. None were abused, and they all had the trappings of a lovely childhood. For all of these people, there was really only one thing seriously wrong. And the thing that was wrong was invisible. It was something imperceptible, something *missing* that no one inside or outside of the family could see.

For a person with Emotional Neglect, the numbness and suffering are held in secret. Like all of the other emotions, they are not shared with anyone else. Over time, you may be able to imagine the toll that this would take on any human being. Like floodwaters over a river basin, they gradually erode away the bedrock of a person's existence: their energy, motivation, self-esteem, and engagement in life.

PART III
FILLING THE TANK

Chapter 5

HOW CHANGE HAPPENS

B efore we start the process of trying to correct what's missing, it's important to take a little time to consider change: how it happens and how it doesn't, what gets in the way, and what to do if it doesn't go as you would like (as it seldom does).

You will see that in the next chapters, I've included a number of Change Sheets. They are intended for you to use in your attempts to fill the empty spaces and address the habits that may have developed out of your Emotional Neglect. These Change Sheets are in no way meant to imply that change is as one-dimensional as a sheet. My concern is that as you go through the chapter, you may feel them to be a cookie-cutter approach to the deeply held, complex, individual struggles with which you are faced.

Taking a factory-created, one-size-fits-all approach is *not* my intention. Such an approach would be doing nothing more than furthering your Emotional Neglect, which is the last thing I wish to do. So as you read through the remaining chapters on **Filling the Tank**, please know that I intend for you to take a buffet approach. Choose the Practice Sheets, techniques and suggestions that apply *to you*, and tailor the Practice Sheets in ways that will be helpful *to you*.

In the meantime, let's talk about some of the most powerful factors which can get in the way of successful change. Understanding them and keeping them in mind as you start to make changes will help you to see them quickly when they come up. It will also help you work through them if they start to hold you back.

Factors That Get in the Way of Successful Change

1. False Expectations

- **That change is linear:** It is natural to expect that, once you start working to make a change, you should see success that gradually builds upon itself, getting better and better over time. Picture a staircase that you are climbing, taking one step at a time, with steady progress upward. Most real change does not work that way at all. Instead, it comes in fits and starts. Two steps forward, one step back. The real key is to just keep working through the backward steps, consistently and persistently, until you take another step forward.

- **That setbacks are failures:** The danger of feeling like you've failed when you have a setback is that feelings of failure can easily turn into self-anger. And self-anger is the enemy of progress. It can easily send you off track or backward.

- **That if you get off track, you may as well give up:** Getting off track is built in to the process of making a change. If you are trying to eat better, exercise, or change any longstanding behavior or habit, there's a very high probability that more than once you will get off track. It is absolutely OK if it happens, and it's immaterial to your ultimate success, as long as you don't give up.

2. Avoidance

Change is difficult on a lot of different levels. First, you have to make yourself do something that feels foreign; second, you have to be able to make yourself do something that you find difficult; third, you have to be persistent, as described above; and fourth, making a change requires a lot of work.

A natural reaction to all four of the above challenges is avoidance. Isn't it pretty tough to take on all of those? Wouldn't it be more comfortable to simply put it out of your mind and not worry about taking on those battles? Of course it would! But, like self-anger, avoidance is the enemy of progress. Avoidance may beckon like an oasis in the desert, but it will leave you parched.

The only way to deal with a natural pull toward avoidance is to face it head on. Take notice of those moments when your avoidance kicks in, then turn around and challenge it. Remind yourself that it will take you down a one-way street to nowhere. Remind yourself that all things worth having require effort. Then pull out your Change Sheet and start working.

3. Discomfort

Change can be a very frightening thing. When you start to feel different from your old self, or when people start to react to you differently because of the changes you've made, it can feel like you're living in an alien world. It's hard to know how to behave and how you should react. Suddenly, things don't feel as safe as they once did.

In my experience, most people are unaware of their discomfort. But they feel it, and then they naturally want to retreat from their changes, and go back to where they were before. This is a completely natural feeling and a very normal response. But it's just as dangerous as any of the factors we talked about above. It sends you back toward square one. For example, many people, after they've lost their first few pounds, suddenly feel different. Even if it feels better, it also feels strange, and that's uncomfortable. So they lose muster and their efforts fade. Be aware of the strong possibility that this might happen for you. Watch for it. Recognize that it's normal but destructive. Don't let it take you down. Just keep going.

Chapter 6

WHY FEELINGS MATTER AND WHAT TO DO WITH THEM

"Although many of us may think of ourselves as thinking creatures that feel, biologically we are feeling creatures that think."

—Dr. Jill Bolte Taylor, Neuroscientist

1. Understanding the purpose and value of your emotions

In our society we undervalue emotion. It's often viewed as a nuisance. Words are frequently applied to it like "sappy," "mushy," or "schmaltzy." Emotion is often thought of as childish, effeminate or weak. It's considered the antithesis of thought. We have a tendency to assume that smart people aren't emotional people, and emotional people aren't smart. The reality is that the smartest people are those who use their emotions to help them think and who use their thoughts to manage their emotions. The key is to use emotion in a healthy balanced way. Listen to what your feeling is telling you, and then figure out a way to act upon it to better your situation, your life, or the world around you. Many of the most valuable scientific discoveries were made because a scientist was passionate about his or her subject. The scientist's passion might be driven by grief, for example, or by a wish to discover a way to help a loved one who's suffering. But most successful people are driven by feeling.

Neuroscientists have studied extensively the evolutionary development of the human brain. For humans, the ability to feel emotion evolved millions of years before the ability to think. Human emotions originate in the limbic system, which is buried deep below the cerebral cortex, the section of the brain where thought originates. In this way, our feelings are a more basic part of who we are than are our thoughts. They're a physiological part of our bodies, like fingernails or knees. Our emotions cannot be erased and will not be denied, any more than we can erase or deny our hunger or thirst, our elbows or our earlobes.

Why did emotion evolve in the first place? Sometimes, especially to emotionally neglected people, emotions feel like a burden. Wouldn't it be better if we didn't have to feel sad when we had a conflict with a friend, angry when someone cut us off in traffic, or anxious before a job interview? On the surface, maybe it would seem easier if we didn't have to feel those things. But my belief is that *if we didn't have emotions, life would not be better. In fact, it would not be sustainable.*

Emotion is necessary for survival. Emotions tell us when we are in danger, when to run, when to fight and what is worth fighting for. Emotions are our body's way of communicating with us and driving us to do things. Here are some examples of the purposes of just a few emotions:

Emotion	**Function**
fear	tells us to escape/self-preservation
anger	pushes us to fight back/self-protection
love	drives us to care for spouse, children, others
passion	drives us to procreate, create and invent
hurt	pushes us to correct a situation
sadness	tells us we are losing something important

compassion	pushes us to help others
disgust	tells us to avoid something
curiosity	drives us to explore and learn

You get the idea. For every emotion, there is a purpose. Emotions are incredibly useful tools to help us adapt, survive and thrive. People who were emotionally neglected were trained to try to erase, deny, push underground, and in some cases, be ashamed of, this invaluable built-in feedback system. Because they are not listening to their emotions, they are operating at a disadvantage from the rest of us. Pushing away this vital source of information makes you vulnerable and potentially less productive. It also makes it harder to experience life to its fullest.

Emotions do more, though, than drive us to do things. They also feed the human connections that give life the depth and richness that make it worthwhile. It is this depth and richness which I believe provides the best answer to the question, "What is the meaning of life?" Emotional connections to others help us stave off feelings of emptiness as well as existential angst.

2. Identifying and Naming Your Feelings

Remember Cal, our example for Alexithymia in Chapter 2? A significant part of Cal's problem was that he had *zero* awareness that his own emotions existed. This is true to some extent (although not always so severely) in all emotionally neglected people. You may recall that Cal's undifferentiated, internalized feelings festered inside of him, emerging only as anger and irritation.

Emotions can do a variety of interesting things when they are pushed underground or ignored. They can:

- become physical symptoms like GI distress, headaches, or back pain
- turn into depression, causing problems with eating, sleep, memory, concentration, or social isolation

- sap your energy
- cause you to explode at random times, or blow up "over nothing"
- aggravate anxiety and/or panic attacks
- keep your relationships and friendships superficial and lacking in depth
- make you feel empty and unfulfilled
- cause you to question the purpose and value of your own life

The first step to stopping (or preventing) any of the above from happening to you is learning to recognize your feelings and put them into words. There is something almost magical about saying, "I feel sad," "I am frustrated," or "You hurt me when you did that." When you identify and name your feelings to yourself or to another person, you are taking the wheel and stepping on the gas. You are taking something from the inside and putting it on the outside. You are making the unknown known. You are taking charge. And you are making the most of a valuable resource: your emotions, your fuel for life.

3. Learning to Self-Monitor Your Feelings

Identifying and putting words to feelings is a skill. Just like any other skill, it has to be worked at, and it requires a lot of effort to develop. Here we will learn an exercise that will help you do just that. When you are first practicing this exercise, it will be important to be in a room alone, free from all distraction.

Identifying and Naming Exercise

Step 1: Close your eyes. Picture a blank screen that takes over your mind, banishing all thoughts. Focus all of your attention on the screen, turning your attention inward.

Step 2: Ask yourself the question:

"What am I feeling right now?"

Step 3: Focus on your internal experience. Be aware of any thoughts that might pop into your head, and erase them quickly. Keep your focus on:

"What am I feeling right now?"

Step 4: Try to identify feeling words to express it. You may need more than one word.

Step 5: If you're having difficulty identifying any feelings, skim through the Feeling Word List in the Resources at the end of this book, and see if one or more words jump out at you.

Step 6: When a feeling word seems like it may be accurate, you are ready to move on to the next step, which is trying to figure out **why** you are feeling that.

So now ask yourself:

"Why would I be feeling _____ right now?"

Determining the reasons behind a feeling can be very difficult for many people, but especially for those with Emotional Neglect. Asking yourself questions about the feeling can help you to understand why you are feeling it. So let's use an example here to illustrate how you might go about this. Let's suppose that the feeling you identified is sadness.

Again, close your eyes again, turn your attention inward, and ask yourself as many of the following questions as needed to develop an understanding of the feeling.

"What is going on in my life right now that might make me feel sad?"

"Has something happened recently to upset me?"

"Has something sad or troubling from the past been brought back up by recent events?"

"Is this feeling of sadness familiar to me?"

"Have I felt this sadness often before?"

"If so, when and why?"

"Is this an underlying feeling that's often with me?"

"If so, what's happened in my past that may have caused it in the beginning?"

This exercise may seem simple, but it is not easy. Emotionally neglected people often have great difficulty sitting with themselves, and that is a requirement for this exercise to work. If it seems very hard when you first attempt it, or even impossible, you must keep trying. Some people have found it helpful to take a yoga or meditation class to help build the internal focus skills that are so important here. You are forcing your brain to perform several activities that are novel. In essence, you are forging new neural networks which get stronger and perform better and better each time you do it, even when you are not successful.

Use the following **Feelings Sheet** as a template to record your feelings at least 3 times per day. The goal will be to gradually become more able to focus inward, so that you will be naturally tuned in to your emotions as they occur. When this awareness starts to happen, you will finally have access to all of the power that your emotions bring you. And you will be released from the destructive, burdensome labor of suppressing them.

Feelings Sheet

*Record your feelings 3 times per day. Use Feelings List from Resources as needed

SUN	Morning	
	Afternoon	
	Evening	
MON	Morning	
	Afternoon	
	Evening	
TUE	Morning	
	Afternoon	
	Evening	
WED	Morning	
	Afternoon	
	Evening	
THU	Morning	
	Afternoon	
	Evening	
FRI	Morning	
	Afternoon	
	Evening	
SAT	Morning	
	Afternoon	
	Evening	

Remember to be sure to tailor this Feelings Sheet to your own needs. As I said before, this is not meant to be a cookie-cutter approach! If it's hard to keep doing it or you fear you're not doing it well enough, please go back and read Chapter 5, **'How Change Happens'**.

Now that you have your emotions, we are ready to learn what to do with them.

4. Accepting and Trusting Your Own Feelings

If you were emotionally neglected, chances are you have difficulty with accepting and trusting your feelings. Some emotionally neglected people are completely unaware of the existence of emotions (like Cal). Others push their emotions down because they have a deep-seated notion that feelings are bad, will burden other people, or can make them a bad person. Remember the following three rules.

1) There is no bad emotion.

Emotions themselves are not good or bad, right or wrong, moral or amoral. Every human being has felt rage, jealousy, hate, destructiveness, and superiority, for example, at one time or another. Most people have even had homicidal feelings. These feelings themselves are not bad, and do not make us a bad person. It's what we do with them that matters. Do not judge yourself for your feelings. Judge yourself for your actions.

2) Feelings do not always make rational sense, but they always exist for a good reason.

Emotions do not follow the principles of logic. They can seem inexplicable and unpredictable. But *every* emotion can be explained if you try hard enough. With every emotion our body is trying to send us a message, no matter how bizarre that may seem. As an example, let's go back to David, the forty-something businessman who had zero supervision as a child. David once shared with me that he occasionally felt an unbearable disgust and repulsion when he saw a random person eating in a restaurant. He was mystified by this feeling, and worried that it might mean he was crazy. Eventually, through a lot of exploration of his Emotional Neglect, we figured out the reason: David's limbic system, unbeknownst to him, was equating eating, the taking in of food, with nurturance. David himself took no enjoyment from food. He had great difficulty letting himself enjoy nutritional nurturance as well as emotional nurturance. Unconsciously, he felt disgusted when he saw someone letting down their guard, and allowing themselves to enjoy taking in nurturance. This is an example of a feeling that seems on the surface irrational and meaningless, but was actually quite meaningful, and existed for a very good reason.

3) Emotions can be very powerful, but they can be managed.

Emotions that are hidden tend to have a lot of power over us. When we are aware of an emotion, we can then take charge of it. David felt at the mercy of his intense feeling of disgust, and sometimes avoided going to restaurants in order to avoid that feeling. Once he realized the source of the feeling and didn't judge himself for having it, he was at a point of full awareness and acceptance. He started to fight it off, and the feeling of disgust lost its potency. Eventually it disappeared altogether.

The IAAA Steps

IAAA may sound like a retirement fund, but it is not. **IAAA** stands for: **Identify, Accept, Attribute, Act**. These steps are a culmination of the three rules above. They are the four steps to maximizing the value of our emotions, and gaining energy and guidance from them. First, **Identify** the feeling, then, second **Accept** it. Do not judge it as bad or good. Third, try to discern the reason you're having that feeling, or **Attribute** it to a cause; fourth, identify whether there is an **Action** that the emotion calls for and, if so, take it appropriately.

What are you feeling right now? Close your eyes, and ask yourself that question. If the answer is "overwhelmed," don't despair. The process of making friends with your emotions may seem complicated, or even insurmountable, but you can do it. Yes, it will take time. But if you keep working at it, you will start to notice small changes in yourself. The changes may be subtle and may at first seem unimportant. But each time that you have an emotional realization that's new to you, it's a sign that you are growing and learning. If you find yourself struggling too much, or on the verge of giving up, I encourage you to look for a therapist to help you. A skilled therapist will be able to help you build these skills, so that you can become fully connected, present and alive.

5. Learning to Express Your Feelings Effectively

Remember, emotions themselves are not bad; it's what we do with them that matters. A very effective way to harness and use the power of our emotions is to express them appropriately. That means not passively, not aggressively, but **assertively** and with **compassion**. The word "assertive" is thrown around a lot in business trainings and seminars. But the word does have a specific meaning. When you express something assertively, you are expressing it in such a way that the other person can take it in. In order to be truly assertive, you must have compassion and empathy, meaning an awareness of how what you are about to say may affect the other person.

Let's say that you're working hard on all of the steps in the Identifying & Naming Exercise, and you're becoming more aware of when you are angry. One day, you're waiting in line at the movies and a sleazy guy cuts the line right in front of you. To handle this situation assertively, you would not keep your anger to yourself; you wouldn't just whisper it to your friend; you wouldn't yell at the guy or call him a jerk (although you may want to). You would tap him on the shoulder, mindful (with compassion) of the possibility of embarrassing him, and say quietly but firmly, "Excuse me sir, but the end of the line is back there." Hopefully he will look sheepish and go to his proper place. But of course it is possible that he will not. The point here is that you express yourself instead of bottling up your feelings so that they may eat away at you from the inside. Although you can't control another person's response, if you are assertive, you will likely, no matter what he does or doesn't do, feel better for having taken appropriate action. And your anger will not be bottled up, only to cause a headache or backache later.

Let's look at another example. Let's say that it's Friday, and you're looking forward to going out with your friend Betsy tonight. Right before you leave work your boss calls you into her office and tells you that she's disappointed with your work on the Chris P. Bacon account. She tells you that you must step it up or she will have to remove you from the account. After laying all this negative feedback on you, she sends you off to "enjoy" your weekend. Your mood has plummeted due to the unexpected verbal thrashing you've just received. You head off to meet Betsy in a black mood.

In this situation, you have a choice to make. Choice #1: You can choose not to tell Betsy about the incident due to embarrassment, or because you just want to put it behind you and enjoy the evening. Choice #2: You can tell Betsy what has just happened.

If you make Choice #1, chances are it will backfire. You will not be able to hide your upset feelings from Betsy, and she probably will spend much of the evening wondering why you're not your usual fun self tonight. You may end up drinking too much, appearing sullen, or taking it out on her somehow.

If you make Choice #2, here's a description of how it might go:

> *"Betsy, I'm so glad we're going out tonight because I really need a distraction. I am so upset. You won't believe what happened at work today. I feel misunderstood, underappreciated and angry." Tell Betsy the story and how you feel about it. Let her offer some possible interpretations, give you some solace, or just listen. After you've had this conversation, Betsy will feel closer to you as a friend. You will feel closer to Betsy. You will have gotten it off your chest, and you will have a far better chance of putting it aside and having a better evening.*

Please note a very important factor here. Betsy did not help you *solve* the problem. She simply listened. The magic of feeling better and coping better lies in putting words to your feelings and sharing them. If you have never experienced this magic, it is extremely important that you try it. If it's too hard to do it with a friend or family, contact a professional therapist or counselor. They are virtually all trained to help you learn this process.

All of the principles described above apply to all emotions, like diffidence, discontentment, or betrayal. Once you have Identified, Accepted and Attributed, then you can Act. You can apply words to the feeling, and express it appropriately. Sometimes, in certain situations, it is enough, or best, to express it just within yourself; sometimes it will be best to talk to a third party who's not directly involved; and sometimes, you'll need to express your feelings directly to the person involved. This is where assertiveness comes in.

There are many good books on assertiveness available. See the Resources section for my suggestion for a book that can help you learn to express your feelings in an assertive and compassionate way.

6. Recognizing, Understanding and Valuing Emotions in Relationships

People who grew up emotionally neglected tend to carry some false beliefs about emotions in relationships. Here's a good, but not exhaustive, sampling:

1. Sharing your feelings or troubles with others will make them feel burdened.
2. Sharing your feelings or troubles with others will chase them away.
3. If you let other people see how you feel, they will use it against you.
4. Sharing your feelings with others will make you look weak.
5. Letting others see your weaknesses puts you at a disadvantage.
6. It's best not to fight if you want to have a good relationship.
7. Talking about a problem isn't helpful. Only action solves a problem.

Fortunately, not one of these beliefs is true. In fact, they are each and every one dead wrong. (The only exception is if you share your feelings with another emotionally neglected person, who may not have any idea how to respond). When you grow up receiving consistent direct or indirect messages that you should keep your feelings to yourself, it is natural to assume that those feelings are burdensome and undesirable to others. This section is about overcoming these assumptions. If you cannot let them go, they will hold you back in every area of your life, but especially in your relationships with others.

First, let's talk about:

Friendships

When you were reading the story above about the boss's criticism and the night out with Betsy, were you finding it hard to accept the premise that talking with Betsy would be a positive thing? If you were actually in that situation, would you keep your troubles to yourself due to some of the seven beliefs listed above (or some of your own beliefs that aren't listed)? If so, there is only one way to learn the real truth, and that is to try what I call:

The George Costanza Experiment.

In the 1990s Seinfeld was probably the most popular sitcom on TV. In one episode, the character George Costanza, who was the quintessential loser, decided to go for an entire week doing the opposite of what he would naturally do. When an attractive young woman asked him where he lived, instead of his usual half-truths and convoluted efforts to imply that he was successful, he said, "I'm unemployed and living with my parents in Queens." This was hilarious, of course, but it also opened up a whole new world for George. He found himself with dates galore and a number of other positive gains.

For our purposes, the George Costanza Experiment would mean doing the opposite of what you would normally do when it comes to sharing your feelings. For example, it would mean telling Betsy your problem to see if it does help you manage your feelings; to see if she uses it against you; to see if she runs away; to see if she is so burdened by it that it ruins her night; to see if it gives her a new view of you as "weak." It would mean letting others see and hear what you're feeling, and watching to see if it brings you harm or help. It would mean daring to fight out a problem with your friend instead of pushing it aside, to see if it is destructive to your friendship.

Nothing is always 100% foolproof in every situation. It is true that some friendships may not be capable of surviving the challenge of building emotional depth, but one could argue that those friendships may not be of high quality anyway. So by and large, if you stick with the George Costanza Experiment, I am very confident that you will find your relationships growing stronger and deeper, yourself feeling calmer and more grounded, and others seeing you as a stronger person, not weaker.

Emotionally neglected people tend to be good listeners. But they are not good at talking, especially about themselves. This cuts them off from a vital source of sustenance in life. After all, emotional connection is the stuff of life, making it worth living. It's the sugar in the beautiful cake. It is the heartbeat of humanity.

Now let's talk about:

Marriage

In my office I have seen couple after couple in which one member expresses grave dissatisfaction with the relationship but cannot explain the reasons. Think back to Trish and Tim, the Achievement/Perfection Focused parents in Chapter 2. Trish said, "When I try to talk to him, he shuts me down. I know he's miserable and I want to help but I can't." Often the unhappy spouse will say, "He's not abusive, he doesn't drink, he makes a good living. But I'm just not happy with him. Something is missing." Some people are able to say that they need more intimacy than their spouse is giving them. But when the spouse asks what that means, they typically have no answer.

What they are actually asking for is a feeling of emotional connection, a feeling that their spouse can read them and that they can read their spouse, that they and their spouse naturally feel each other's feelings. Since emotional connection is the stuff of life, it is both the glue that holds a relationship together and the fuel that keeps it burning. A relationship in which there are no fights is a relationship that will fizzle and die out. Couples who are truly emotionally connected let each other know when they are hurt, get angry, and fight things out when needed. This willingness to be vulnerable keeps passion alive and prevents visits to the therapist's office or the divorce court.

Everything you read above about friendships also applies to romantic relationships except more so. Friendships can be maintained by common interests alone, at least for a while. A romantic relationship doesn't just require emotional connection; it rests upon it. Feelings are the foundation of romance, love, and a lasting relationship.

Here are my suggestions for building emotional connection in your marriage:

1. Practice the Identifying and Naming Exercise daily
2. Follow the IAAA Steps
3. Work on using assertiveness with compassion with your spouse
4. Ask questions! Ask your spouse questions, listen to his or her answer, and ask more questions. See below.

Horizontal and Vertical Questioning[1]

Not all questions are the same. Some questions have more power than others. People who are emotionally tuned in seem to naturally know how to ask powerful questions. They know what to ask in order to get to the heart of a matter or of a person. Emotionally neglected people, for reasons we have talked about, do not typically have this skill unless they cultivate it for themselves.

One way to get to the real heart of a matter or of a person is to practice vertical questioning in addition to horizontal questioning. Horizontal questions are questions aimed at getting *information*. Vertical

1   Sharon Jacques, PhD., Psychological Care Associates, Couples Training Seminar, 2002

questions are aimed at *understanding*. For example, let's say your husband comes home from visiting his elderly mother and appears glum. Your first question would naturally be, "How did your visit go?" He says in response, "Good."

Examples of **Horizontal Questioning** in this situation would be:

Q: How's your mom?

A: She's OK

Q: Did she get out today?

A: She went to the store.

Q: Did she like the soup I sent last week?

A: She did.

Q: Does she seem OK?

A: As good as she usually is.

Q: Does she still seem depressed?

A: She's always been a little depressed.

Q: Did you tell her about Suzy's dance recital tomorrow night?

A: Yep.

Notice that in this exchange, your horizontal questions have gained you a good deal of desired information. You have discovered that your mother-in-law is OK, liked your soup, is no more depressed than usual, and is aware of Suzy's dance recital. Horizontal Questioning is very useful for information gathering and exchange. I estimate that it constitutes over 90% of all of the communication that goes on between people.

But there are some situations in which Horizontal Questioning falls short. This might be the case if you are trying to understand a person or her experience on a deeper level, or delve deeper into a issue. In the following example, we're going to go back to your husband returning home after visiting his mother. But this time, you are looking for an answer to a more complex question. You want to know why your husband seems glum, and to find out, you're going to need to query him vertically.

Here is an example of how you would use **Vertical Questioning** in this situation:

Q: You seem glum. Was everything OK with your mom?

A: Do I? Yeah, she's fine.

Q: You always seem down after seeing her lately. What's going on?

A: (Pause, appearing thoughtful) Do I? I didn't realize that.

Q: Did she say anything that upset you?

A: No, I don't think so.

Q: What do you think it is about going to see her that makes you glum?

A: (Pause, appearing thoughtful again) I dunno, maybe it's just seeing her looking so old. I'm not sure how much longer she'll be around. She just seems so weak. I worry about her living alone.

Presto. Vertical Questioning has helped your husband see himself through your eyes, think more deeply into himself and his feelings, put his feelings into words and share them with you. Now that his feelings are out on the table, you can listen, help him process them and *use* them. Maybe his emotions are telling him that it's time to start taking more steps to care for her. Maybe they're telling him that he should start preparing himself to lose her.

In true Vertical Questioning, it is vital to listen to the other person's answer. Your next question should be geared toward pushing their attention inward and driving them deeper into their emotions. It must always be done with care and compassion. If you do it right, it will help you get to the heart of the matter and of the person.

The steps I've outlined in this section may make it seem that recognizing, understanding and valuing emotions in relationships should be easy. But it is not. It's very difficult, even for people who have not been emotionally neglected. If you or your partner has been emotionally neglected, you will have to work much harder, and you may need assistance through various steps. Please see the **Resources** section for my recommendation of an excellent book by Terrence Real which offers couples understanding and assistance with emotional connection.

I know you're probably not keen on asking for help. But I hope you'll consider letting a professional help you if you run into difficulties or get stuck as you go through the process of developing these skills, as well as the ones ahead in Chapter 7: Self Care.

Chapter 7

SELF-CARE

There are four major ways in which the emotionally neglected tend to fall down when it comes to taking care of themselves and their own needs, and for good reason. Adults who were emotionally neglected as children often don't know what their needs are. Their own wants, needs, and feelings are not only irrelevant to the emotionally neglected, they're invisible. The four major areas we'll talk about here are:

Part 1. Learning to Nurture Yourself
Part 2. Improving Self-Discipline
Part 3. Self-Soothing
Part 4. Having Compassion for Yourself

All four of these skills tend to come naturally to people who received *enough* nurturance and discipline from their parents during childhood. If your parents had *enough* compassion and empathy for what you were feeling as a child, you will have the same for yourself as an adult. If your parents had *enough* closeness, caring and acceptance in their relationship with you as a child, you will most likely have a good capacity for intimate relationships as an adult.

When you grow up emotionally neglected, these abilities which seem to come somewhat naturally to others become skills which you have to develop in adulthood. Developing a skill takes work. It requires time and conscious effort. In this chapter, we'll talk about what these skills are, what they mean and how to cultivate them for yourself. At first each skill may feel foreign and clumsy as you try it. The key is to keep at it, no matter how it feels. This is one of the few times that I will tell you to ignore your feelings! All skill development requires persistence, and I promise you that persistence will pay off.

As you read about the skills in this chapter, you'll see that I've devised a special tracking sheet, called a **Change Sheet** for all but one. In working on these skills and using the Change Sheets, please be aware that if you try to work on all of the skills at once, it could be overwhelming. I recommend that you master them one skill at a time, and preferably in the order I've presented them here. At most, try to take on two at once. Don't start on another one until you've mastered the one before it. And if one of them doesn't seem to apply to you, then by all means skip it and go on to one that does seem fitting. Be sure to pace yourself, as it's better to put all your effort into one skill than to spread yourself too thinly over multiple ones.

All of the skills we'll be talking about in this chapter are challenging to master. Many, many people spend years of their lives trying to gain control over them. It's important to give yourself plenty of time, understanding and *care* as you use the **Change Sheets.** Take pride in your accomplishments. When you get off-track, don't be angry at yourself; just get yourself back on.

Most likely, you will need some help as you go through this chapter using the **Change Sheets**. Throughout the process, please use my website, www.drjonicewebb.com, as needed for ongoing support, tips and assistance.

Self-Care Part 1. Learning to Nurture Yourself

You may be wondering exactly what this means. The word nurturance could have a number of different meanings. Here, I am talking about self-nurturance as taking the steps that are necessary to help yourself have a healthy, enjoyable life. If you are healthy and enjoying life, it will open you up to have a positive impact on the people around you. Your health and happiness will have a ripple effect that will spread to your spouse, children and friends and continue outward. As an emotionally neglected person, you may already be an excellent caretaker *of others*. Now it's time for you to start paying attention to your own needs and taking care *of yourself*. There are four steps to learning to nurture yourself. They are:

Step A: Putting yourself first
Step B: Eating
Step C: Exercise
Step D: Rest and relaxation.

Self-Nurturing Step A: Putting Yourself First

Let's start with putting yourself first. What? Did I hear you say that's selfish? It is not! When you are healthy and strong, you're freed up to give to others in a richer, deeper, healthier and stronger way. I like to think of it this way: during the flight safety announcements that we rarely listen to, the flight attendant cautions that if oxygen masks drop in front of each seat, adults should secure their own mask before helping others. This request makes perfect sense. You will not be effective in putting on your child's mask when you are struggling to breathe yourself. This rule applies to life in general. Once you're secure and solid yourself, you can help others much more effectively.

When you first start to work on putting yourself first, you may encounter resistance. Surprisingly, it will be primarily from the people closest to you. Think about it this way: all of the people who know you best expect you to behave a certain way. For example, they know you will say yes when they ask you a favor. The first time you say no they'll be taken by surprise. They may feel miffed, and they may convey that to you in some way. Please keep in mind that this is the normal process of change. Change doesn't come easily to the changer herself or to her loved ones, even when it's a healthy and positive change. Sometimes it helps to explain to the people closest to you that you're working on better self-care and that you may be doing some things differently from now on. It may be an adjustment, but anyone who truly cares about you will eventually adjust with you, and will probably even come to respect you for it.

To learn how to better put yourself first, it may help to have some guidelines, which I've listed below. As you work on building this skill, you may find some of the guidelines easier to follow than others. As you read them, be sure to think about which ones you may need the most help with. I've included a **Change Sheet** to help you to work on each one separately.

<u>Learn to say no.</u> No doubt, the people in your life know you pretty well. They know that you will be there for them, because that's what emotionally neglected people do. Your copious amount of compassion *for others* makes you feel obligated to say yes to requests from your friends, family, children, boss. Of course, there is nothing wrong with saying yes. It's essential for positive relationships and progress in life. The problem comes when you feel that unless you have a really good excuse to say no to a request, you must say yes. As a result, you may end up sacrificing yourself too much by saying yes to things that you don't actually have the time or energy for. It's very important to free yourself from this quandary so that you can make decisions that are best for yourself, while also taking others' needs into consideration.

A primary rule of assertiveness is that anyone has the right to ask you for anything; and you have the equal right to say no, without giving a reason. If everyone operated this way, feeling free to ask for help when needed and feeling free to say no when desired, the world would be a better place. Boundaries would be clearer, and there would be a lot less unnecessary, useless guilt floating around. If you feel guilty saying no, or if you find yourself saying yes to things because you're uncomfortable saying no, please get a good book on assertiveness (there are many available; see the Resources page in the back of this book for my recommendation) and start trying to overcome it. Saying no when you need to, free of guilt and discomfort, is a vital building block of self-care.

Reading a book on assertiveness will help you understand and embrace the concept so that hopefully you can change your own philosophy. But after you change your philosophy, you must follow that up by changing your behavior. Use the **"Saying No" Change Sheet** on the next page to track on a daily basis the number of times you say no to requests that are overly-demanding of you.

"Saying No" Change Sheet

*Record number of times you say 'no' per day

	Jan.	Feb.	March	April	May	June	July	Aug.	Sept.	Oct.	Nov.	Dec.
1												
2												
3												
4												
5												
6												
7												
8												
9												
10												
11												
12												
13												
14												
15												
16												
17												
18												
19												
20												
21												
22												
23												
24												
25												
26												
27												
28												
29												
30												
31												

As I've said before in this book, the more you do something that's foreign, the less foreign it becomes. Gradually, over time it will become a normal process and seem to happen on its own with little effort on your part. The point of this **Change Sheet** is not necessarily to increase the quantities, since each day will offer a different number of situations in which it's actually appropriate to say no. It's meant more to help you keep overall track of the changes in your behavior. It will also help remind you every day to work on it. It's harder to forget that you're working on saying no when you know that you'll have to record it that evening.

Ask for help. Asking for help addresses the counter-dependence that can be so ingrained in the emotionally neglected person. Remember David, our example of counter-dependence in Chapter 3? David had internalized his parents' message, "Don't have feelings, don't show feelings, don't need anything from anyone, ever," and he was living his adult life according to it. When you've spent your entire life unaware that relying on others is not only an option but a necessity, it's very hard to see it any other way.

There's another aspect of asking for help that's difficult for the emotionally neglected to deal with. If it's hard for you to say no, chances are it's hard for you to ask for help as well. Assertiveness works both ways. Emotionally neglected people often live their lives trapped in a Catch-22. Since you feel that you must say yes when someone asks you for a favor or help, or even extends a social invitation, you naturally assume that others feel the same way. Since you don't want to put others in that bind, you don't feel comfortable asking them for a favor or help. In a world where, in your head, nobody can say no to anyone, you are going to lose. These ways of thinking make you available to help others but unable to ask others for help when you need it. Can you see that this is a no-win system for you?

To free yourself from this difficult bind, all you have to do is accept that other people don't feel guilty or uncomfortable saying no. Other people have an intrinsic understanding of this rule of assertiveness. The huge majority of people have little angst about asking for help and little angst about saying no. As soon as you can join them, a new world will open up for you.

Use the following **"Asking for Help" Change Sheet** to track and make yourself aware of your efforts to ask for help more often.

"Asking For Help" Change Sheet

*Record number of times you ask for help per day

	Jan.	Feb.	March	April	May	June	July	Aug.	Sept.	Oct.	Nov.	Dec.
1												
2												
3												
4												
5												
6												
7												
8												
9												
10												
11												
12												
13												
14												
15												
16												
17												
18												
19												
20												
21												
22												
23												
24												
25												
26												
27												
28												
29												
30												
31												

Discover your likes and dislikes. When you were growing up, perhaps your preferences were not considered often. Questions like "What do you feel like doing today?" "Would you rather go to a pizza restaurant or a hamburger place?" "Do you want to buy this shirt in green or pink?" "How do you feel about that?" Emotionally neglected adults can have great difficulty knowing themselves. Remember Josh from Chapter 3, with the unrealistic self-appraisal? Josh had received so few questions like this in his childhood that he had no idea as a college student what he was interested in, what he liked, or what would be a fitting college major. Depending on the amount and types of interest your parents showed you growing up, you may have certain areas where you know yourself well, and certain areas in which you're mystified. Here are some questions to help you figure out where you're lacking in knowing your likes and dislikes:

- What's your favorite kind of food?
- What's your favorite sport to play?
- What's your favorite sport to watch?
- Do you even like sports?
- Do you have a fashion sense? If so, what's your style?
- What's your favorite way to spend a Saturday?
- Are you in the right job/career for you?
- What's your favorite movie genre?
- What kinds of books do you like to read?
- Can you name a talent that you feel you have and would like to cultivate in yourself?
- If you could travel anywhere in the world, where would you go?
- Do you have enough friends?
- Do you enjoy the friends you do have?
- Which friends do you enjoy the most?
- What comes naturally to you?
- What's your least favorite chore?
- What's your least favorite activity?
- What things take you the most time to accomplish?

I could go on and on with these questions, but let's stop here. If you can easily answer most of them, good for you. If you struggled through, it's definitely an indication that you've been focused outward for much of your life (as you were trained to do in your childhood) and have not been tuned in to yourself. An important part of caring for yourself is knowing what you like. Knowing what you like will help you define what you want. Then when your spouse or friend says to you, "Where should we go for dinner, Italian or Greek?" you'll have an answer for him or her. In sharing your answer, whether the other person agrees or not, you are taking an important step in taking care of yourself.

Use the following **"Likes and Dislikes" Change Sheet** to write down everything you can think of that can be categorized as a like or a dislike. It may include places, colors, foods, activities, furniture styles, people, people's actions, or your own moods, for example. Anything at all that you can categorize, write it down on the sheet. Then, as you go forward, day by day, write down things as they occur to you. Tracking and writing down your likes and dislikes as you discover them will help you not only be aware of your own feelings about things, it will also help you own those feelings. There's no right or wrong to your likes and dislikes. They simply are what they are, and they are valid and important.

"Likes and Dislikes" Change Sheet

Likes	Dislikes

Put a higher priority on your own enjoyment: When you were growing up emotionally neglected, you probably didn't have great latitude to make choices to bring yourself enjoyment. Quite possibly other people's wishes came before your own. Or, if your family was scrambling for resources, there wasn't much left for fun things. If you grew up with any type of emotionally neglectful parents, chances are you place far too little value on your own experience of pleasure and fun as an adult. To change this there's only one option, and it involves putting yourself first.

In some ways, this last guideline encapsulates the first three. In order to put a higher priority on *your own* enjoyment, you have to say no to requests that pull you too far away from it. You have to ask for help sometimes so that you feel enough support and connection to others to be available to the opportunities that are out there. And you need to know what you like so that you can seek it.

Again, you may be wondering, "If I put myself first in order to seek enjoyment, won't that make me selfish?". Keep in mind that everyone needs and deserves enjoyment. You deserve it as much as anyone else does. Sometimes you'll have to say no to one person in order to free yourself up to have fun with another. This is not about selfishness, it's about balance, balance between giving and receiving; balance between self and others. Don't be afraid of making decisions that put your fun on a higher priority. The emotionally neglected are at far smaller risk of becoming selfish than are most people. As someone who has been trained to put your own needs, wishes and desires to the side, you have an extremely far distance to go before you could become selfish.

When putting your own pleasure last is so deeply ingrained, making a decision to change it will not be enough. That decision is an important first step, but it must be followed up with action. Can you see where this is going? It's another **Change Sheet, "Prioritizing Enjoyment."** You'll find it on the next page to help you track and stay aware of your need to work on making different choices. If you keep working at it, over a period of time, it will start to feel less foreign. Your brain will start making the

"Prioritizing Enjoyment" Change Sheet

*Record number of times you prioritize your own enjoyment per day

	Jan.	Feb.	March	April	May	June	July	Aug.	Sept.	Oct.	Nov.	Dec.
1												
2												
3												
4												
5												
6												
7												
8												
9												
10												
11												
12												
13												
14												
15												
16												
17												
18												
19												
20												
21												
22												
23												
24												
25												
26												
27												
28												
29												
30												
31												

choices on its own, and it will become second nature for you. At some point along the way, you may be surprised to find that life is starting to feel less mundane and tedious.

It's good that you're working on putting yourself first! Because you will need to be better at that in order to make progress on eating, exercise, and rest/relaxation. These all address the physical part of nurturing yourself. They're all about what you put into your body and how you expend your energy.

Self-Nurturing Step B: Eating

Not all emotionally neglectful parents neglect their children in this area. But as we've talked about before, it's possible for parents to provide their children with plenty of food and still manage to emotionally neglect them in the area of eating. It is a parent's responsibility to help his child develop a healthy relationship with food. Many parents who are not emotionally neglectful fail to do this with their child simply because they don't have a healthy relationship with food themselves. They are unable to teach what they do not know. But emotionally neglectful parents fail in the eating area for the same reasons they fail their children in other areas.

Before we talk more about eating, please answer the questions below about your **adult** eating habits.

1. If you have a spouse or children of your own now, do you often sit down and have meals together?
2. Do you pay attention to nutrition and try to make sure that you eat a balanced diet?
3. Do you keep too much junk food in the house?
4. Do you eat more junk food than you should?
5. Do you still have a preference for "kid food," like hotdogs, chicken nuggets or pizza?
6. Do you make sure to have plenty of vegetables and fruits, i.e., some with every meal?
7. Are you a good cook?

8. Are there times when there is literally no food in the house for a meal?
9. Do you eat a lot of frozen or pre-packaged prepared food?
10. Do you sometimes forget to eat?
11. Do you tend to overeat?

Do not read on until you've answered each of the above questions yes or no. Once you're finished with those questions, please move on to answer the questions below about your **childhood** eating experiences.

1. When you were growing up, did your family sit down and eat meals together often?
2. When you were growing up, were your parents careful about making sure you got a balanced diet?
3. When you were growing up, was there a lot of junk food, such as chips, cookies, ice cream, candy, or sweets in the house?
4. If so, did your parents closely supervise how much of the junk food you ate and when you ate it?
5. Were you raised on hotdogs, chicken nuggets and pizza?
6. Did you usually have a vegetable or fruit with every meal?
7. Was at least one of your parents a good cook?
8. Were there times when there was literally no food in the house for a meal?
9. Did your family eat a lot of frozen or pre-packaged prepared food?
10. Did you skip meals as a kid?
11. Did you tend to overeat as a kid?

You probably noticed that some of the questions in the adult section match up directly with the questions in the childhood section. Go back and check your answers. What we're looking for here is the extent to which your adult eating habits match up with your childhood eating experiences. Consider childhood as the programming phase of your life.

Most of us in adulthood tend to follow the programs that we were set up with as a child. For an example of this, think back to third-grade Zeke, whose Permissive mom threw him a football and offered him ice-cream to help him feel better about the note from his teacher. Any parent might use food to help a kid feel better here and there. But if Zeke's mother uses this often, or even just at the wrong times, she'll inadvertently teach him to use food to manage his emotions. In adulthood, he may have a tendency to continue this. This could cause him to eat the wrong things for the wrong reasons, none of which is healthy.

Most people as adults greatly underestimate the extent to which they are influenced by their parents' programming of them as children. As adults, we experience ourselves as making free choices, our own decisions. The reality is, the program we were set up with by our parents in childhood is incredibly powerful. While it's not easy to override these programs, it certainly can be done. You've probably found that some of your childhood answers from the eating questions don't match the adult ones. These are the programs from your childhood which either you have overcome on your own, or have been altered by other life experiences.

As an emotionally neglected person, there may be some aspects of eating which your parents didn't teach you at all. In these areas you had no choice but to fill in for your parents and program yourself. To illustrate this, let's go back to Noelle from the 'Little Compassion for Self' section in Chapter 2. Noelle microwaved herself a frozen chicken sandwich every morning for breakfast all through middle and high school. Since no parents were attending to her need for fresh, healthy food, Noelle was forced to figure out something for herself. Her childish solution became her program. This program continued to run when I met Noelle; as an adult, she and her husband and children subsisted almost solely on a combination of frozen food and take-out. This illustrates the way in which the emotionally neglected child's self-program is just as persistent and powerful as the one that comes from his parents.

By answering the childhood and adult eating questions were you able to identify some areas in your relationship to food that are not healthy?

Have you been struggling to change those habits already? If so, that's understandable. Our childhood programs are not at all easy to change. By the time we reach adulthood they've become more than just habits, they've become ways of life. Changing a way of life is difficult but it is certainly possible. It just takes work. I hope that realizing how your problem eating areas are rooted in your Emotional Neglect will stop you from self-blame and decrease your frustration. It's important not to waste your energy on any of that, and to instead put your energy into having compassion for yourself and making changes.

To override your unhealthy programming, you'll need to use many of the Emotion skills you learned in Chapter 6, and many of the Self-Care skills you've already learned in this chapter. Be aware of your feelings, accept them and share them with others. This will help you avoid eating for emotional reasons. Say no when you need to. Ask for help, and use the help you get. Prioritize your enjoyment so that you won't rely upon food excessively for reward and pleasure. And use the **"Eating" Change Sheet** to change the aspects of your eating that you identified as problems in this section. And again, a reminder to be careful to avoid trying to change too many habits at once.

"Eating" Change Sheet

*Record the number of times each day that you override an unhealthy habit

	Jan.	Feb.	March	April	May	June	July	Aug.	Sept.	Oct.	Nov.	Dec.
1												
2												
3												
4												
5												
6												
7												
8												
9												
10												
11												
12												
13												
14												
15												
16												
17												
18												
19												
20												
21												
22												
23												
24												
25												
26												
27												
28												
29												
30												
31												

Self-Nurturing Step C: Exercise

Despite the clear and consistent research findings showing that physical exercise is a primary aspect of improved health, the majority of Americans are not doing it. According to the Centers for Disease Control and Prevention in Atlanta, only 35% of adults engage in regular leisure time physical activity (2009). There are all sorts of reasons why people do not act upon the best advice of doctors and health researchers. It helps greatly to have these three basic building blocks for a lifetime of healthy exercise habits: you realize and understand the value and importance of exercise; you have found a form of exercise that's enjoyable to you; you are good with self-discipline.

Now that you understand more about Emotional Neglect and about the programming that takes place in childhood, you can see how the emotionally neglected might have extra challenges in any or all of those three areas.

Depending upon your age, you may or may not have had the opportunity to learn about the *value* of exercise. It's certainly possible that your parents didn't know this themselves because much of the research has been conducted in the last twenty years or so. Generally anyone over 30 years old may have learned about the health benefits of exercise themselves rather than from their parents. Not having been taught the importance of exercise is not in itself a sign of Emotional Neglect. But if you don't realize its importance, you're unlikely to make it happen.

If you were not emotionally neglected in this area, you stand a much better chance of having enjoyed in childhood a sport or physical activity that you might carry over into adulthood. For example, if your family went on weekend trips skiing or hiking, or if your family supported you in playing *and enjoying* a sport like baseball, football or tennis, you're more likely to have grown up appreciating the enjoyment that can come from physical exercise. When you find exercise enjoyable, it's much easier to prioritize it as an adult.

Self-discipline is probably one of the largest hurdles that gets in the way of emotionally neglected people's exercise habits. In Chapter 3 we talked about William, whose single mother gave him an unstructured childhood by not making him do things that he didn't want to do. When you grow up with discipline that's either too harsh or too lax, you do not get the opportunity to internalize the ability to discipline yourself in a healthy way. You don't learn how to make yourself do things that you don't want to do, in this case, exercise. As you read on to the next section in this chapter you'll learn much more about self-discipline.

To evaluate your standing in these three areas of physical exercise, let's start by answering some questions about your **adult** life:

1. Do you believe that exercise is important?
2. Would you describe yourself as active?
3. Do you enjoy playing one or more sports?
4. Are you able to force yourself to exercise when you don't feel like it?
5. Have you discovered one or more types of physical activity that are enjoyable, for example, aerobics, hiking, running, swimming, weight-lifting, bike-riding?
6. Should you exercise more than you do?
7. Do you struggle with self-discipline in general?

Don't move on until you've answered yes or no to each of the seven questions above. Once you've answered all of the questions, please move on to answer the questions about your **childhood** below:

1. When you were growing up, do you think your parents believed that exercise was important?
2. Would you describe yourself as having been an active child?
3. As a child, did you enjoy playing one or more sports?
4. As a child, did your parents make you go outside to play or do something else active sometimes when you didn't want to?
5. As a child, did you enjoy active play?

6. Do you believe that you should have had more exercise than you did as a child?

7. Were your parents either too lax (permissive) or too strict (authoritarian, for example) with discipline in general when you were growing up?

Since you've already been through this in the section on eating, it will be easier for you to see the meaning of the correspondence between your answers in the childhood and adult sections. If you see from your answers that you're active enough and have no problems in this area, then congratulations, you are one of the 35%. Perhaps this is one of the ways in which your parents came through for you, or perhaps you've managed to set up your own healthy habits for yourself. Either way, you're in good shape.

If you've been able to identify some specific aspects of exercise that you need to work on, be sure to read *Self-Care Part 2, Improving Self-Discipline*. Also use the **"Exercise" Change Sheet** to work on changing your behaviors so that you can nurture yourself in this way too.

"Exercise" Change Sheet

*Put a checkmark on the days that you exercise

	Jan.	Feb.	March	April	May	June	July	Aug.	Sept.	Oct.	Nov.	Dec.
1												
2												
3												
4												
5												
6												
7												
8												
9												
10												
11												
12												
13												
14												
15												
16												
17												
18												
19												
20												
21												
22												
23												
24												
25												
26												
27												
28												
29												
30												
31												

Self-Nurturing Step D: Rest and Relaxation

So now that we've talked about Putting Yourself First, Eating, and Exercise, it's vitally important to pay attention to your ability to Relax. I have found that most emotionally neglected people fall into one of two categories: they either rest and relax too little, or they rest and relax too much. Some switch back and forth from one to the other with little balance. Let's take a moment to look at how Emotional Neglect can cause this sort of imbalance.

A parent who's in tune with her child can tell when her child is hungry and makes sure to the best of her ability that her child eats. Such a parent also sees when her child is tired, and makes sure to the best of her ability that the child gets some rest, *whether the child wants to rest or not.* Furthermore, an aware and observant parent does not make her child rest when it's convenient for the parent; she makes the child rest either on a regular schedule, which teaches the child to routinely and consistently take care of himself; or she makes the child rest when it's clear that the child needs it. This teaches the child how to read his own signs of tiredness and how to make himself rest when he needs it. Through this process of parental observation and emotional attunement followed up by action, a child has the opportunity to internalize all of these skills for himself. As an adult, he will be in tune with his own body. He will know his own signs of tiredness, whether they be crankiness, quietness, silliness, fogginess or something else, and when he observes them in himself, something will click in his head that says, "OK, you need some R & R." And then he'll do his best to see that he gets some rest, *whether he wants to rest or not,* just as his parent did for him in childhood. Notice that a part of this scenario is that he may have to make himself do something he doesn't want to do, which is a separate but related skill.

All children can be lazy sometimes. It's an attuned parent's job to notice when a kid is going overboard with this and push the child to engage in activity *whether the child wants to or not.* A six-year-old shouldn't be allowed to watch TV for hours, nor should a teen be allowed to lay in bed all day listening to her iPod. Neither of these is good for the child. Parents who allow this too much are probably doing it for their own benefit. Out of sight, out of mind. If the child isn't underfoot or causing a problem, the parent can be freed up. Of course no parent is perfect at this; it all boils down to whether he does it *well enough*. If the parent does not do it *well enough*, the child may, as an adult, have difficulty forcing herself to get up *whether she wants to or not*.

Let's take, for example, the Narcissistic and Sociopathic Parent Types. These parents, as talked about in Chapter 2, have a tendency to put their own needs above those of the child. In these situations the parent makes the child rest at a particular time because the parent is tired and needs a break. Or the converse, the parent doesn't allow the child time to rest when the child needs it because it's not convenient for the parent. An Authoritarian Parent might misread a child's tiredness as disrespect, i.e., lack of love and be offended or hurt by it; Divorced/Widowed, Addicted, Depressed, Workaholic, Caretaker of Ill Family Member, and Well-Meaning all might allow the child to languish or exhaust themselves out of pure obliviousness; Permissive simply avoids conflict so doesn't get involved to this level in the child's needs. Achievement Parents may place their need for the child to study or practice the violin over any honest physical need that the child shows.

In all these cases, the child is not getting what she needs. She is not learning her own physical cues; she's not getting the message that rest is important when she's tired or that too much rest is bad for her. And she's not learning how to override her own impulses, which is a vital part of self-discipline.

As an emotionally neglected person, it's important for you to determine where your parents may have failed you, well-meaning or otherwise, and correct it for yourself. Are you someone who can over-indulge in rest? Do you not rest enough? Do you bounce back-and-forth between those two extremes? If so, please use the **"R&R" Change Sheet** to start learning to attend to and regulate your needs for rest. Also, read on to the next section on Self-Discipline, as it's an important part of being able to self-regulate.

"Rest & Relaxation" Change Sheet

*Put a checkmark on the days that you rest & relax

	Jan.	Feb.	March	April	May	June	July	Aug.	Sept.	Oct.	Nov.	Dec.
1												
2												
3												
4												
5												
6												
7												
8												
9												
10												
11												
12												
13												
14												
15												
16												
17												
18												
19												
20												
21												
22												
23												
24												
25												
26												
27												
28												
29												
30												
31												

Self-Care Part 2. Improving Self-Discipline

No doubt you have noticed the term "self-discipline" sprinkled throughout this book. That is because it is a very common issue among the emotionally neglected. Although there are a number of possible underlying causes of self-discipline struggles, like depression or attention deficit disorder (ADD), I often have found it to be Emotional Neglect. Many people who were emotionally neglected freely describe themselves as procrastinators. Some call themselves lazy. Common are battles with over- and under-eating, excessive spending, or over-drinking. As mentioned above, many emotionally neglected people also have difficulty forcing themselves to exercise, do menial tasks or do anything that's not immediately fun or rewarding.

This may sound like a big list of unrelated items. Actually, they all boil down to the same thing: *making yourself do things you don't want to do and stopping yourself from doing things you shouldn't do.* This is one of the classic dilemmas of the emotionally neglected.

After reading about William's struggle with Self-Discipline in Chapter 3, and the Eating, Exercise and Rest & Relaxation sections of this chapter, you probably have a general sense of why this is. Human beings are not born with an innate ability to regulate and control themselves. These are both vital skills which lucky people learn in their childhood. Here's how:

When your mother calls you in from playing with your neighborhood friends because it's dinnertime or bedtime, she is teaching you this important skill. She's teaching you that some things must be done, even if you don't feel like it. When your dad gives you the weekly chore of cutting the grass and then follows up in a loving but firm way to make sure you do it, he's teaching you how to make yourself do what you don't want to do and he's teaching you the rewards of that. When your parents make sure you brush your teeth twice a day, when they say no to dessert, when they set aside and enforce "homework hour" every day after school because you've been slacking on homework, when they continue to love you but set your curfew earlier as a consequence of thoughtlessly breaking it; all of these parental actions and responses are internalized by you, the child. You not only internalize the ability to make yourself do things and to stop yourself from doing things, you internalize your parental voices, which later in adulthood become your own.

The internalized parental voice is extremely important, and it can often go awry in Emotional Neglect. Let's take the example of William from our Self-Discipline section of Chapter 3. William's busy single mother loved him dearly. She let him run relatively free throughout his childhood with little responsibility at home and low accountability at school. William was an intelligent, likeable, even charming boy, and everyone wanted the best for him. His teachers cut him slack because they could see that he was bright and capable. William would later report a fun, free childhood and be perplexed by his adult struggles with being productive and confident. His wife was confused by his difficulty regulating his eating, sleeping and work hours. She was puzzled by his erratic tendencies, such as working into the wee hours of the morning, sleeping a few hours, skipping meals, then going to bed at 7 p.m. the next night. But William's productivity suffered not just because of his erratic schedule. It also was compromised by a harsh voice in his head when he was working which frequently told him that what he produced wasn't good enough, wasn't done quickly enough or would be a disappointment to his boss. William spent so much time and energy battling this harsh, critical voice in his head that he had little left over to produce much of anything.

You may be wondering where William got this harsh inner voice. After all, his mother was not harsh with him. She didn't judge him or give him negative feedback or expect too much from him. The problem was that in the *absence* of a parental voice, William had to make up his own. He not only had a shortage of skills for structuring himself so that he could be productive, he had no idea what he could expect of himself or how to judge the quality of his productions. The voice he invented for himself was not a balanced, moderate and loving adult voice. His inner voice went back and forth between harsh judgments and complete indulgences. This is why his wife was puzzled by his erratic sleep hours, eating habits and work schedule.

William's inner self-regulating voice was erratic, both harsh and indulgent. Some emotionally neglected people's self-created voices are more predictable, meaning they are only one or the other. Still other emotionally neglected people actually manage to figure out self-regulation for themselves, and create a voice for themselves that's mature, measured, caring and firm. If you are in this last category, you can give yourself all the credit for a job well done. If you're in one of those previous categories, do not despair. You can change your self-discipline voice. As an adult, you can re-parent yourself in this area by basically rewiring your own brain. You can do it by using a simple but effective rewiring program I call **The Three Things Program**.

In this skill-building exercise, you will be wiring your brain with the hardware that's essential to have in order to be able to make yourself do what you don't want to do and vice-versa. It works like this: **<u>Every day, you must do Three Things that you don't want to do or stop yourself from doing Three Things you want to do but shouldn't</u>**. Every day, you record the Three Things on your, you guessed it, **"Self-Discipline" Change Sheet.**

"Self-Discipline" Change Sheet

*Record your 'Three Things' each day

SUN	Morning	
	Afternoon	
	Evening	
MON	Morning	
	Afternoon	
	Evening	
TUE	Morning	
	Afternoon	
	Evening	
WED	Morning	
	Afternoon	
	Evening	
THU	Morning	
	Afternoon	
	Evening	
FRI	Morning	
	Afternoon	
	Evening	
SAT	Morning	
	Afternoon	
	Evening	

To help you get a feel for this, I'll give you some examples of Three Things that my patients have done and shared with me. They are: face-washing, bill-paying, exercise, floor-sweeping, shoe-tying, phone-calling, dishwashing and task-starting. On the "things you stop yourself from doing" side: not eating a piece of chocolate devil's food cake, not buying a pretty necklace online, not having that one more drink when out with friends, and not skipping class. Keep in mind that the point here is not to deprive yourself of enjoyment. If chocolate cake isn't a problem for you, then that may not be the impulse to override. Try to choose urges that are negative for you in some way.

As you can see, it doesn't matter how big or small the Thing is. It's not the Thing that's done or not done that really matters in this exercise. It's the action of overriding your default setting. It's a bit like the George Costanza Experiment in that you're forging new neural pathways in your brain by forcing yourself to do something that's not supported by the current neural connections. Try to do this program regularly. If you slip, start right back up again without being too self-critical and without being too self-indulgent by letting yourself off the hook. If you keep at it, you'll notice that it will become easier and easier for you to self-regulate, manage your impulses and complete unrewarding but necessary tasks. It will build and grow and eventually become an active, hard-wired part of who you are.

Self-Care Part 3. Self-Soothing

No matter how good you get at the IAAA Rules (Identify, Accept, Attribute, Act) for managing your emotions, you will undoubtedly have times in your life when you will be emotionally uncomfortable. As you know from having lived thus far, life hands us all kinds of experiences. And in response to those experiences, we have all kinds of emotions, some wonderful, some neutral, and some unpleasant. IAAA will certainly help at those times. But what do you do when the feeling is persistent or difficult to manage? This is where self-soothing comes in.

As an emotionally neglected person, chances are good that you haven't put much thought into the concept of self-soothing. Self-soothing is another life skill that non-neglected children learn from their parents. When a father rubs his fitful son's back to help him fall asleep after a nightmare, when a mother holds her crying child and smooths his forehead, when a father listens carefully to his daughter's long story about something unfair that happened to her at school that day, when a mother sits with calm quiet empathy through her son's tantrum, these emotionally present parents are teaching this vital life skill to their children. Children whose emotions are accepted, tolerated and appropriately soothed internalize their parents' ability to do so. Children absorb the self-soothing skill like the little sponges that they are, and it's a skill that they'll need to have throughout their entire lives.

You probably didn't grow up completely devoid of all soothing from your parents. Again it comes down to whether you received *enough*. Many emotionally neglected people as adults are improvising in this area.

"A story? Honey, wouldn't you rather a mild sedative?"

Just as no two people are exactly the same, no two people are soothed the exact same way. Everyone's needs are different. Throughout my career as a psychologist, I've helped people identify a seemingly infinite number of different self-soothing techniques.

The worst time to try to figure out what works for you is when you need it the most. It will work very much to your advantage to identify good possible strategies and have them ready to try when you do need them. It's likely that a self-soothing strategy that works in one situation may not work in another and vice-versa, so it's good to have not just one strategy but a list of them. That way, in your moment of need, you can try one and if that doesn't work, try another.

In order to identify effective soothers, it may help to think back to your childhood. Were there things that you found comforting as a child? Also, think back to the most emotionally challenging times of your adulthood. Have there been helpful self-soothing strategies that you've used in the past without realizing it? One warning is to be careful what types of strategies you use. Make sure they're healthy for you. Alcohol, shopping and eating can help in moderation but if they're over-used they can make your problem bigger later. Or they can end up giving you another problem to deal with.

Below are some examples of healthy self-soothing strategies that have been identified and used effectively by others. Try these and/or use them as a starting point to help identify what works for you and make your own list.

- bubble bath
- long, hot shower
- listen to music; may be a particular song
- polish your car
- exercise; run, lift weights; take a bike-ride
- play guitar or other instrument
- cook or bake (we're talking about the process here; be careful not to over-use food itself for self-soothing!)

- spend time with your pet
- play with a child
- go for a walk
- a smell that you found comforting in childhood
- call a friend
- lie on the ground and watch the clouds or look at the stars
- clean
- go to the movies
- sit quietly and look out the window
- sit in a church and meditate
- **self-talk**: Self-talk is probably the most useful and versatile of all self-soothing strategies. It involves literally talking yourself through your uncomfortable feeling state. You can do it quietly, on your own, within your own mind, so you can do it in public, in a meeting or on a train. Remind yourself of simple, honest truths which will help you keep things in perspective. Here are some examples of things you can say to yourself:

    "It's only a feeling, and feelings don't last forever"

    "You know you're a good person"

    "You know you meant well"

    "You tried your best, and it didn't work out"

    "Just wait it out"

    "This will pass"

    "I need to figure out what I can learn from this, and then put it behind me"

The possibilities are endless, and must be determined by the situation and by what you're feeling. This self-soothing strategy works for most people. It is definitely worth adding to your repertoire.

Use the **"Self-Soothing" Change Sheet** on the next page to make your list. Be sure to keep your list flexible. Scratch off ones that stop working for you and add new ones as needed. Make self-soothing a meaningful, purposeful endeavor that grows and changes with you. All of your life you will need to have the ability to soothe yourself. As you get better at it, you'll find yourself a calmer person who feels more in control and more comfortable overall.

Self-Soothing List

1.

2.

3.

4.

5.

6.

7.

8.

9.

10.

Self-Care Part 4. <u>Having Compassion for Yourself</u>

You may be either disappointed or relieved to learn that there will be no **Change Sheet** to help you build your self-compassion. That's because this aspect of self-care is actually more of a feeling and a philosophy than a skill. It will be much more difficult to build it by changing your behavior, or in other words from the outside in. It is best developed from the inside out.

That said, I did save self-compassion for last for a reason. It's a higher-order aspect of self-care. If all of the components of self-care were put into pyramid form, self-compassion would be at the top. It rests upon all of the self-care skills you've been working on above. It requires a level of self-love and kindness that can only come when you care enough to treat yourself well.

Why is self-compassion so important? If you have a lack of compassion for yourself, you're more likely to castigate yourself with a ruthless internal voice for your own honest mistakes and errors, like Noelle and William did in Chapter 3. You may go so far as blaming yourself and being angry with yourself for having normal feelings and issues, like Laura in Chapter 3, or you could even end up feeling worthless and empty to the point of considering suicide, like Robyn in Chapter 4.

No matter how you slice it, judging, blaming, disliking, insulting and wanting to kill yourself are all the opposites of self-care. Chances are you wouldn't treat anyone else this way, so why do you treat yourself this way? All of these are self-destructive and will exhaust your energy reserves and take you nowhere but down.

Remember that compassion, along with empathy, is one of the highest forms of human emotion. It's healing, soothing and unifying. It pulls people together and holds them in a positive and compelling way. The compassion you have for others is a part of the positive effect you have on the people and the world around you. It's time that you yourself receive some of the benefits of that. Here are five guiding principles to help you in your quest to increase your self-compassion.

Self-Compassion Principle 1.
The Golden Rule in reverse

"Do unto others as you would have them do unto you" is the Golden
Rule. The Golden Rule for the emotionally neglected is the same
rule, but in reverse. "Do unto yourself as you would do unto others."
In other words, don't let your critical voice say anything to you that
you wouldn't say to someone you care about. Don't punish yourself
in a way that you wouldn't punish someone you care about. If you
wouldn't punish a friend for doing something, don't punish yourself
for it either. Do you think that if your friend ran over a curb while
parallel parking, you would say to her, "You idiot, what a lousy driver.
You're an embarrassment"? No, you would not. You should therefore
not speak to yourself that way. If you find yourself unable to silence
your harsh Critical Voice, I highly recommend the book _Self-Esteem_
by McKay & Fanning.

Self-Compassion Principle 2.
Become aware of damaging self-directed anger

Anger at yourself is the opposite of compassion. Start trying to notice
how often and how intensely you feel angry with yourself. This is
important because there is a point at which self-directed anger becomes
unhelpful. It starts to make you dislike yourself as a person and that's
self-destructive. If you make a mistake, there's only one thing you can do
and that's learn from it. Anything else is wasted energy. Any time you feel
angry with yourself, consider it a cue to turn the compassion you have
for others upon yourself.

Self-Compassion Principle 3.
Give yourself the benefit of your own wisdom and compassion

As an emotionally neglected person, you're probably a great listener.
And like Robyn from Chapter 4, your friends talk to you because
you give them helpful advice. You're nonjudgmental, caring and
compassionate _to others_. That's a breeze for you. Your job now is

becoming able to use your own voice of nonjudgmental wisdom to help yourself the same way that you use it to help others. That means being able to *speak your wisdom to yourself* and being able to *listen and take in your own voice.* Why should others get the benefit of your help and caring, but not you?

Self-Compassion Principle 4.
Develop an inner loving-but-firm voice

As an emotionally neglected person, you didn't get the advantage of internalizing a loving-but-firm voice from your parents. While other kids' parents were saying, "It's OK, let's figure out what to do so that you'll do better next time," you were scrambling for yourself. You were, in the absence of helpful parental input, saying to yourself either the too harsh "You idiot" or the letting-yourself-off-the-hook, "I'm not going to think about this." With the former, you're feeding self-anger and draining off your energy; with the latter, you're setting yourself up to make the same mistake again. Either way, you lose.

A helpful, positive loving-but-firm voice will seem like a dialogue, in that you are questioning yourself, making yourself think, in a *nonjudgmental* way, about what went wrong and how to prevent it from happening again in the future. Here's an example of what your voice might say to you if you forgot to fill up the car and ran out of gas on the freeway on the way home from work.

> *"How did this happen? You were going to stop and fill up after running errands at lunch today!"*
>
> *"Well, let's see, why didn't I stop and fill up after lunch today?"*
>
> *"Oh, yes, I was running late. I barely made it back for my 1 o'clock meeting because there was such a huge line at the Department of Motor Vehicles."*
>
> *"Those were really circumstances out of my control. How can I make sure this doesn't happen again?"*

"Never plan gas fill-up for lunch time. There's not enough flexibility in that one hour to make sure it will be done."

"From now on I'll make sure I gas up either during the morning driving to work or on my way home so I won't be set up to forget again."

Notice how this loving-but-firm voice isn't too easy on you but neither is it self-destructively tough. The voice takes four key steps. It:

1. holds you accountable for your mistake without jumping to judgment or blame
2. helps you think through which part of the mistake is your fault and what part is due to other people or circumstances
3. determines what to do differently to prevent this error from happening again in the future
4. helps you realize that you've learned something important from this mistake and lets you *put it behind you*

These steps are all productive and useful. They're the means to an end. They will help make your life better without doing damage to your self-esteem or your self-confidence. All of life is about learning, growing and becoming better. These three steps will do all of those things for you. Keep working on creating that loving-but-firm parental voice.

Self-Compassion Principle 5. Allow yourself to be human.

Like having feelings, making mistakes is an essential part of being human. Both are non-negotiable conditions of humanity. Please know that there's not a human being on earth who hasn't had many, many feelings and made many, many mistakes. If you meet people who say otherwise, don't listen to them; they're full of nonsense (to put it kindly).

No doubt working on all of these skills must seem a bit daunting. Having lived a childhood devoid of some of the most important components of emotional health and self-care leaves you with no choice but to re-parent yourself in your adulthood.

My solemn promise to you is that if you do this work of building yourself up, brick by brick, skill by skill, step by step, you'll reap the tremendous rewards. As you build up the pyramid of self-love, you'll be climbing it too, until you reach the top and find that you have a level of kindness and calmness within yourself and for yourself that you never knew existed. And when you turn your powerful compassion upon yourself, you'll be living with a new You. A You that's loveable, fallible, imperfect, with strengths and weaknesses, wins and losses, sensitivity and resilience. A full and connected You.

Chapter 8

ENDING THE CYCLE: GIVING YOUR CHILD WHAT YOU NEVER GOT

"I swore I wouldn't make the same mistake with my children as my parents did with me."

I f you were emotionally neglected and are a parent or want to be one someday, it's very important that you read this chapter carefully. The first thing we'll address here is your own parental guilt. Second, together we'll identify the areas in which your Emotional Neglect challenges appear, or may appear in your future as a parent. Finally, we'll talk about what you can do to make sure that you will be an emotionally attuned parent who raises children who are emotionally aware and attuned to themselves and others.

But before any of that, let's start with the good news. Take heart that no matter what mistakes we've made as parents, they can be fixed. Children are incredibly resilient. As I've said before, children are like little sponges. They soak up whatever we give them. And the converse is also true; they don't soak up what we don't give them. So as soon as we change what we're giving them, they'll change, often after an adjustment period. Beyond that, any changes you make in yourself will trickle down to your children. The more you change yourself for the positive, the more your children will naturally change for the positive. This is true even for teenagers, although teens can be somewhat different because they'll often do their best to hide those changes from you, their parents. Don't be fooled. Your teen is changing too.

1. Your Parental Guilt

Here's my first question for you: Has reading this book made you doubt or feel guilty about your parenting? Has it set off that self-blame and ruthless self-judgment that's so typical of the emotionally neglected? If so, please absorb the principles below before you read on. As you continue through the chapter, be sure to return to these five principles and reread them as needed to address any guilt that may arise for you. This will require you to be emotionally attuned to yourself so that you'll notice when you feel guilty. And emotionally caring for yourself so that you'll take the time to come back and read them again.

- Many parents have some degree of guilt about their parenting at times. It often arises out of concern about whether you are doing the job right. But guilt is NOT NECESSARY for good parenting, and it can actually interfere with healthy parenting.

- If you're a guilt-prone parent, your guilt may be interfering with your ability to make good parenting decisions. It's hard to say no when you feel guilty. It's harder to set limits with your children. It can make you second-guess your every move. Children pick up on parental self-doubt and know how to take advantage of it. Therefore, guilt weakens you as a figure of authority.

- While guilt may be a sign that you care, you will probably be a better parent without it. Instead of feeling guilty, the goal is to hold yourself accountable as a parent, but also understand that no parent is perfect. All parents make mistakes, including at least a few big ones.

- Try to follow the same rules for parenting that you follow for self-discipline. If you're harsh on yourself for your parenting mistakes, you're sapping your own energy and rendering yourself weak and ineffective. Holding yourself responsible is not the same thing as kicking yourself.

- Like everyone else, you've been parenting according to what you've known and experienced yourself. You haven't been able to offer your own children the emotional strengths that you didn't have yourself. The fact that you're reading this book (and this particular chapter) means that you care and that you're ready and strong enough to change. You already have a great advantage over your own parents.

2. The Changes You Have Made So Far

Perhaps you've already been making some changes in yourself as you've been reading this book. If you have, then your children already may have had some reactions to those changes. Are you saying no more often? Are you more often putting yourself first? Are you making your own enjoyment a higher priority? These are all healthy changes for you that will also have positive affects for your children. Unfortunately, they may not realize that quite yet. Children just react when they don't get what they want. But that doesn't mean that it's bad that they didn't get what they wanted. They'll benefit greatly from seeing you value yourself and your own needs. It will enable them to grow up valuing themselves and their own needs.

Your child will need help adjusting to the changes you've made. And you will need to combat the effects of Emotional Neglect that may have trickled down from you to them. If you see your child reacting to the changes you've made, try not to react to her reaction. Instead, dive *underneath* her behavior by asking yourself, "*What is she feeling right now?*" Then gently feed it back to her, like this: "*I know you're not used to me saying no about this, Honey. I'm sorry, I know it must be hard for you when I start making different decisions.*" This will not stop her from being upset about your saying no. But you'll be amazed at how much it helps when you simply validate her feelings. More about this later.

3. Identify Your Own Specific Parenting Challenges

The best way to know how your Emotional Neglect is affecting your children is to go back to look at how it's affected you. Whatever holes or gaps you have in your emotional health will be the same holes or gaps that your children will be more likely to have, unless you fill them. Let's look again at the list of adult characteristics that emotionally neglected people are often left with. As you read through the list, put a check mark beside each item that you identified with as you read Chapter 3.

1. **feelings of emptiness**
2. **counter-dependence**
3. **unrealistic self-appraisal**
4. **no compassion for self, plenty for others**
5. **self-directed anger, self-blame**
6. **guilt and shame: what is wrong with me?**

7.   fatal flaw (if people really know me they won't like me)
8.   difficulty nurturing self and others
9.   poor self-discipline
10. alexithymia: poor awareness and understanding of emotions

If you're not sure about a particular characteristic, please go back and read about it in Chapter 3. Don't over-think it; listen to your gut. This is not about what you *think*. It's about what you *feel*. Ask yourself *if you feel that this particular issue applies to you*. You must trust your feelings on this, and that will have an added bonus of being good practice for you in learning to trust your feelings more in general.

Now that you've identified the adult characteristics of your Emotional Neglect, let's talk about how each of these plays out in the context of parenting.

1. Emptiness vs. **Filled With Premium Grade**

Empty feelings arise from not having been filled up emotionally as a child. Something was missing in your connection with your parents, a fullness in the quality and/or quantity of emotional connection as a child. Let's think of the quality of your family's emotional connection as a fuel grade. A child who grows up with *enough* regular octane or above will probably not have a problem with emptiness as an adult.

If you received lower-grade fuel as a child, and you are experiencing emptiness as an adult, there's a good chance that you may not be providing your own children with *enough* high octane fuel. If this rings a bell for you, it's very important to realize that *this is not your fault*. You can't give your child what you don't have yourself. Also it's important that you know there is a solution to this dilemma. It's not a simple formula; it's not a checklist, and it has nothing to do with changing your behavior. In fact, *the only way to give your child what you don't have yourself is to provide yourself with what you don't have*. Only then can your child benefit.

Here's how it works. As you work on all of the exercises presented in Chapter 6 designed to teach you to value your emotions, you will become a more connected, expressive and richly aware human being. As you go through the Chapter 7 change process, you'll be increasing the octane level of your own tank. The richer your own fuel becomes, the richer the fuel you'll be filling your children with. The more you care about yourself, love yourself, understand yourself, and value your emotional self, the more you'll care, love, understand and value your children and their emotions. Gradually you'll have less empty feelings, and gradually your children will become less prone to emptiness. Their tanks will be filled with rich, long-burning, premium grade love for self and others that will keep them going for their entire lives.

2. Counter-dependence vs. **Mutually Interdependent:**

If you have this adult characteristic, it means that at some point you received a message from your parents that it's not acceptable for you to depend upon or need other people. Your own parents' lack of attention to, lack of tolerance for, or failure to fulfill your emotional needs sent you a clear message that you'd better be *fiercely independent*. You'd better avoid needing attention or help. You'd better provide for yourself.

Now take a moment to ponder this question: can you think of any ways in which you might be giving this message to your own children as you raise them? Given that you've grown up valuing fierce independence, it would make sense that you'd value teaching your children to be this way. Or maybe you haven't thought about it at all, and you just automatically do what you know, as all parents naturally tend to do. Either way, you're setting your children up to miss out on the great advantages of being mutually interdependent with their fellow human beings.

"What the heck is mutual interdependence?" you might say. Mutual interdependence is the ideal balance for relationships between adults, be they marriage or friendship (I am excluding parent/child relationships because a tremendous amount of dependency is naturally built into the parent/child relationship.) Mutual interdependence means that both parties in the relationship are capable of a healthy level of independence and self-reliance, but each member of the relationship relies on the other for some things and at some times. Each person is maximized in their potential to care for themselves, but maximized even further by the addition of what the other person has to offer.

If you give your children the message that they are not to depend on others, you are depriving them of the valuable strengths which the other people in their lives can bring them. These strengths could be any way in which another person enriches or enlivens us or lessens our burden. Just a few simple examples from the vast sea of possibilities might be comforting words and a soothing touch, help moving furniture or a well-cooked meal. There must be a balance in our lives that allows us to give and take, love and be loved, care and be cared for. It's mutual Interdependence. And you and your children deserve to have it.

As a parent, how do you raise your children with this kind of balance that doesn't come naturally to you? The reality is, it's not easy. The good news is that the changes you make in your own counter-dependence will trickle down to your children. The less afraid you become to rely on others, the less afraid your children will be to rely on others. But here's the most important aspect of that: the more you're there for your children *when they need you* the more mutually inter-dependent they will be. Don't be afraid of making them too dependent. The only way to do that is to help them too often, in too many ways, when they *don't* need help.

In order to be there for your children when they need you but not overdo it, you must be in tune with your child. Remember third-grade Zeke's Sociopathic mom, who sent him to his room to write "I will never get in trouble at school again" fifty times in cursive? She was an extreme example of a parent who's out of tune with her child's capabilities. A mother who has such a skewed view of what her child can and cannot do developmentally will be a poor judge of when to step in to help her child.

So to be able to distinguish correctly when you should provide your child with help, it will help to follow the example that was given in Chapter 1, *Healthy vs. Emotionally Neglectful Parenting*, which also used third-grade Zeke. You must **feel an emotional connection** to your child so that you'll know when it's time to step in and soothe and help him; you must **pay attention** to your child to give you a good idea of what he truly can and can't do, so you'll know when he genuinely needs help; you must **respond competently**, which means providing him with meaningful and appropriate help.

No parent is perfect at all of these steps. All you can do is try your best. If you do, your children will love and appreciate you in a different way, because they'll feel that you understand them and that they have support and help when they need it. They'll be more willing to reach higher, have richer relationships, and better fulfill their own potential. They'll be both independent and able to take in help from others. They'll feel less alone in the world throughout their entire lives.

3. Unrealistic self-appraisal vs. **Strong, Clear Sense of Self**

This adult characteristic basically comes down to not really knowing who you are. Remember how we talked about children learning about themselves by seeing themselves reflected in their parents' eyes? That reflection is hard to catch when your parents aren't looking at you much. If you as an adult have a view of yourself that's not clear or not based in reality, it probably means that your parents didn't do *well enough* at paying attention to you. This may mean that they didn't spend enough time with you, but not necessarily. A parent can be with their child 24/7 (not that that would be healthy) and still not be seeing his child. **Paying attention** in this case doesn't mean pouring juice as needed. And it doesn't refer to the artful placement of a pretty hair barrette. It means noticing your child's natural likes and dislikes and strengths and weaknesses, remembering them, and feeding them back helpfully to the child. This is how a child internalizes a realistic sense of who she is.

One of the **Change Sheets** was on *Likes and Dislikes*. This sheet was designed to help you become more aware of the things you innately enjoy and don't enjoy. Likes and dislikes feed into self-appraisal, as do abilities, appearance, personality traits, intellect, social skills and preferences, habits, and the almost endless factors that make up who you are. The process you use to learn your likes and dislikes can also be used to learn more about the complexities of who you are. And that process also applies to your parenting.

As you parent your children, it's important that every day you pay attention, and that every day you give them helpful feedback. This doesn't mean being overly critical or negative because that can be damaging to their self-esteem. But if you see your son excelling at football far more than baseball, you can say, for example, "You are a football machine!" You should not say that to him about baseball if it isn't true. But you shouldn't say, "You're not good at baseball," because that's too negative and could be damaging.

Reflect back to your child the academic skills with which she naturally excels. Reflect back the skill with which she tends to struggle, for instance, "We need to spend more time on math." If your child seems to have little talent on the violin but loves to play it, point out to him that you admire his love of music and his willingness to work hard to master something. Avoid giving feedback that's too harsh or might hurt your child's feelings. Avoid giving feedback that's not realistic. Be honest and loving, caring and clear.

Sometimes you have to just be there, observe and say nothing. Your child will absorb your watchfulness and will see his own reflection. During the eighteen-plus years that you're raising him, he'll look into his parental mirror again and again. He'll see this piece of himself and that piece of himself. He'll see the pieces grow, change and develop. The pieces will coalesce into an accurate reflection of a full and complete person, and that person will know what he wants and what he's capable of. He will be starting his adult life with a tremendous advantage that you didn't have: a full, clear and strong picture of who he is. That is a gift only you could give him.

4. No compassion for self vs. **Compassion**

As a parent, you do not want your children to grow up treating themselves harshly, kicking themselves for their own mistakes. You want your child to learn from his mistakes, to keep growing and loving himself. It's your job to teach your child compassion for others and for himself. To do this, you can apply the same four Self-Compassion Principles that we talked about in Chapter 7. If you have compassion for your children, they will have it for themselves and others.

Remember that the first Compassion Principle is the Reverse Golden Rule. Here's how it applies to parenthood:

"Do unto your child as you wish your parents had done unto you."

A parent who grew up emotionally neglected cannot follow her default settings for parenting. Since her default settings were determined by her primary caregivers, those settings will likely result in her passing down her own Emotional Neglect to her child. As a parent, it's vital to work hard to override your own settings and create healthier ones for your child. So when your child makes a bad decision, screws up, does something thoughtless or wrong, it will be important for you to do your best not to react immediately. Impulsive, emotional reactions will be determined by your default settings. Instead, take a moment and think: If I were my child, what would I need from my parent right now so that I can learn from this and move on?

The second Self-Compassion Principle, when applied to parenting, involves watching and responding when you see your child being hard on himself. If you see your child punishing himself for his mistakes or being excessively angry with himself, it's time to step in and help. Point out that his anger at himself is excessive and misplaced. Even if it doesn't seem to help him in the moment, it will plant a seed in the back of his mind that will grow. Then use your self-soothing skills to comfort your child so that he can internalize them.

The third Self-Compassion Principle is to give your child the benefit of your wisdom and compassion. In order for your child to learn to forgive herself, she must experience forgiveness from you. She will internalize the level of harshness that you deliver to her. This encapsulates both of the previous principles because it involves responding to your child's mistakes by appropriately holding her responsible, intervening when you see her being too harsh on herself, helping her understand her mistake and the situation and, in the end, forgiving her. When you do all of these things for her, she'll learn to do them for herself.

Helping your child develop an inner loving-but-firm voice, the fourth Self-Compassion Principle, is vital to helping her have compassion for herself. Remember the example given in Chapter 7 of the healthy internal voice to use after running out of gas? That's a good template to use for your children as well. In the role of parent, talk through what happened and why, and help her determine for herself where she went wrong. Then reassure her that the point of making mistakes is to learn from them. Walk her through the process of understanding, owning, learning and forgiving. This process is extremely valuable and will set your child up to be able to provide the support and accountability that's vital to being a successful and strong adult who has love and compassion for herself and others.

5. Guilt and shame vs. **Healthy Self-Acceptance**

Remember what causes guilt and shame in the emotionally neglected? It's the absence of parental acceptance and validation of the child's feelings, which eventually causes the child to feel that something is wrong with him for having emotions. Since everyone has emotions, the child may eventually become ashamed of this part of himself, trying to hide them from others and even from himself. What then, as a parent, can you do to make sure this doesn't happen for your child? Accept and validate his emotions, of course.

As a parent who was emotionally neglected yourself, this may be more difficult than it sounds. It will require you to become more comfortable with emotions in general. You will need to be tolerant of what your child is feeling, even if you think your child's feelings are excessive or incorrect.

Here are some suggestions for how to understand and accept your child's emotions. To illustrate this, let's think of your child's feelings as water flowing from him.

- If you put a barrier in front of the flowing water, the water will have to go somewhere. It will go around or over the barrier, or eventually, if it has nowhere to go, it will reverse and head back toward the source (meaning your child will turn his emotions upon himself). No matter what, the water will flow somewhere. *You cannot stop the flow of your child's feelings.* So please don't try.
- In order to deal with flowing water, you have to let it flow while you go to the source. So when your child is feeling something, let his feelings flow while at the same time trying to get back to the original cause of the feeling. This may involve asking your child some questions to help you both understand, or thinking back to situations that might have caused or intensified these feelings.
- Watch out for the danger of letting your child's feelings flood himself and you. Although it's not advisable to try to stop your child's feelings, there is a time to step in to help him manage them. Stopping and helping to manage are not the same thing. It's the difference between "Big boys don't cry" and "Let's figure out together what's going on here and what we can do about it."
- Keep in mind that your child's feelings are a basic part of him, rooted in his human anatomy. He must not get a message from you that he's not to have them, but he must learn from you that it's possible and necessary to manage them.
- Use the emotion management skills from Chapter 6 to help your child learn these essential skills.
- Use emotion management skills for yourself, and your child will also learn them by example.

If you do your best to follow all of the principles of emotion management above, you'll teach your child the opposite of guilt and shame. You'll be giving him essential skills that he'll use in every area of his life. He'll get the message from you that his feelings are a normal, healthy part of his identity; that he should listen to what they're telling him, but that he is not at their mercy. As a result, he'll grow up accepting, and even valuing, this vital, connecting, and enriching part of himself.

6. Self-blame vs. **Forgiving**

Forgiving is the final stage of Self-Compassion. When your child makes a poor choice or mistake, you will use the Compassion Principles to help her understand what part of her mistake is herself, what part is someone else and what part is the circumstances. Then you'll help her figure out how to correct her mistake and prevent it from happening again. Then you'll help her forgive herself and put it behind her.

You will put all of this time and energy into your parenting because you have personal experience with what happened for you when your parents didn't. You realize from your own experience that if we don't move on from the many mistakes we'll make in our lifetime, we'll become stuck in them. If we don't forgive ourselves, our mistakes can become an unnecessarily large part of us. They can take over our sense of self, and can even become who we are. You don't want your child to be defined by her mistakes, as perhaps you have been by yours. Teach her that final step: how to *put that mistake behind her.* Then her mistakes will stay in proportion to reality, and she'll be freed up to take appropriate risks in a healthy way while keeping her self-esteem and self-love intact.

7. Fatal Flaw vs. **Likable and Lovable**

You probably remember that the Fatal Flaw is a feeling of being damaged somehow: "If you get to know me well enough you won't like me." It runs rampant in the emotionally neglected because of the *absence* of positive affection and notice from their parents. I can't tell you how many emotionally neglected adults, when asked if they grew up *feeling* loved, will answer, "I always *knew* my parents loved me." Knowing is not feeling, and feeling is the key here.

It is vital to make sure that your child not only knows but *feels* that you like and love her. Warm, caring hugs, laughter, and truly enjoying your child's personality all go a long way toward conveying that *feeling* to your child. I know this may sound like Parenting 101, but this is one of those things that many emotionally neglected people grew up without enough of. And if it doesn't come naturally to you, you may have to cultivate it for the good of your child.

To take it one step further, an essential step in preventing your child from carrying the Fatal Flaw is to deal with your own. The Fatal Flaw is one of those characteristics which seems to be transferred from parent to child almost by osmosis. It seeps through from the parent to the child unnoticed and unrealized, becoming a part of the child's identity, just as it is of the parent's. Because it's a complex and underground emotion, people seldom are aware that they have it, and they certainly can't put it into words. Instead, it's an ever present feeling that drives many of their decisions and hangs over them like a black cloud (remember Carrie in Chapter 3). But the bottom line is if you don't feel this way about yourself, you won't have to worry about the osmosis factor.

I hope that in reading this section, it has been clear how much your feelings about yourself percolate through to your children. If you *feel* love for yourself, you have a much greater capacity for *feeling* love for your child. If you have a strong sense of self-worth, it will seep through to your child, who will also have self-worth. The main point is: when you deal with what's missing inside of you, those absences will not be transferred to your children.

8. Difficulty nurturing vs. **Giving and Caring**

When you were growing up emotionally neglected, you probably experienced gaps in the nurturance you got from your parents. Perhaps you were cared for very well in some areas, physically, for example, but not in others. Nurturing is like a warm type of caretaking. It's giving paired with care. Remember Dave, who had such a hard time with nurturance that he resented his daughter for making him care about her? Dave was, as we talked about, like a sponge too long away from water. His emotional self had become dry and brittle, so he had great difficulty taking anything in and giving anything out.

Your job now, as a parent who had spotty nurturing at best from your parents, is to make sure that your child never runs dry. Every special thing you do to make sure your child feels taken care of sets him up to be able and willing to give that to others. You will want your child to have the best possible success in his own marriage and with his own children. If you give him plenty of warm caretaking throughout his life, he will have it in copious amounts to give to the people he loves.

Here are some ideas to help you provide your child with emotional nurturance:

- Spontaneously give your child a hug when you notice he looks sad.
- Ask her if she's OK if you think she might be upset.
- Spend extra time with your child when you feel he needs it.
- If your child is going through a transition, or any difficult phase, e.g., school starting or ending, a move, change of friends, etc., talk about it with her and do something special for her to show that you notice what she's going through.
- Be aware in general of what he is feeling. Help him become aware of his feelings and put words to them. Accept and validate those feelings. He will experience all of this as nurturing.

9. Poor self-discipline vs. **In Control**

As we talked about before, your own struggles with self-discipline quite likely reflect something about the discipline you received from your parents. Children left to their own devices will quickly learn to indulge themselves. They may also learn how to be quite hard on themselves. They may learn to call themselves lazy, a procrastinator or a shopaholic. What they will *not* learn is how to make themselves do what they don't want to do, and how to stop themselves from doing what they shouldn't do. Your child will not learn this either, unless you give her what you have trouble providing for yourself: structure, clear rules, and appropriate, predictable consequences.

Structure: When you provide structure for your child, you're teaching him how to structure himself. For example, bedtime is 9:00 on school nights. That's a reasonable rule. As you set and enforce it with your child, you're teaching her how to set a rule in her own head and follow it. Another example might be an hour of homework after school before she can go outside. This forces her to override her own impulses at your behest. When she's older and has control over her own time, she'll carry that ability to overrule her impulses with her. If she can structure herself, she'll be far less likely to procrastinate.

Rules: Once you've set up a structure for your child that's firm but reasonably flexible, it's really important to make that structure clear to your child. To some extent self-discipline is the ability to set clear rules for oneself and then make oneself follow them. That's what healthy discipline involves in your role as parent. Make sure the rules are clear, age-appropriate and easy to follow. Post them on the refrigerator, announce them in family meeting. Don't change them without reason or without informing your child. Your child must know clearly what's expected of him.

Consequences: Your child must know what will happen if he breaks a rule. "If you don't take out the trash on Tuesday, there will be hell to pay" doesn't work. "If you don't take out the trash on Tuesday, I'll take away your iPod until you've done it" does work, because the consequence is clear. "If you don't take out the trash on Tuesday I'll give your iPod to charity" doesn't work because that consequence is inappropriately harsh. It doesn't fit the crime. Your consequence has to be both clear and appropriate, and, on top of that, it must be reliably delivered. The delivery of the consequence can't depend upon whether you're paying attention or have the energy to give it. Your child needs to know that you mean business and he needs to know what to expect from you. Anything less will teach him nothing other than how to break rules and how to have problems with self-discipline.

10. Alexithymia vs. **Emotionally Aware**

During your reading of this book you may have realized that emotional awareness is one of the greatest gifts that you can give your children. You want your child to know what she's feeling and why, and be able to put it into words. You also want her to have skills for figuring out what other people are feeling and to be able to somewhat deduce the reasons for others' feelings and actions. These are important aspects of what Daniel Goldman calls *Emotional Intelligence*. Scientific studies conducted by Goldman show that high Emotional Intelligence is a greater predictor of success than is high intellectual intelligence. Emotionally intelligent people have a huge advantage in navigating the world. This includes the workplace as well as marriage, social situations, and parenting.

Knowing how important these skills are, how do you make sure that your child has them? First of all, everything we've talked about in this chapter will contribute to your child's emotional awareness. But on top of that, there is more that you can do.

Your child will learn little, if anything, about emotion in school. This part of his education is up to you. Here are the five steps to follow to teach your child about emotion so that he'll have a high level of emotional awareness:

1. Pay attention and notice what your child is feeling.
2. Make an effort to feel what your child is feeling.
3. Put the feelings into words for her and teach her how to use her own words to express her feelings. Use the Feeling Word List in the Resource Section as needed to help you with this.
4. Use your Vertical Questioning skills to help him understand the reasons for his feelings.
5. Make emotions an important part of life. Keep emotional language in your everyday vernacular. This alone will convey the value and importance of emotion to your child and will stimulate her interest in understanding the *feeling* part of life.

As you were reading this section, did you start to feel guilty? Did you judge yourself for not doing everything right? If so, it's understandable. It means that you are just like many other caring parents. No parent is fault-free. Every parent falls down in some of these areas. Every parent struggles, and every parent fails at times. As an emotionally neglected parent, you have added challenges. You must have compassion for yourself, learn from your mistakes and continue to put in the effort as you move forward.

If you were able to identify the areas in which your Emotional Neglect affects you and read in this chapter what to do about it, there's a tremendous possibility that you'll be able to correct these issues for your children. Children are amazingly resilient, so they bounce back well. Teenagers are slower to respond to parents' changes, but they do respond. You can't give in to your default settings. You must fight the fight for your own sake as well as for the sake of your children.

Parenting is one of the greatest privileges we are accorded as human beings. No matter what hand we are dealt, it's our biological and social imperative to deal an improved hand to our children. It's our job to reshuffle the cards, and take more time and care than our parents did to give our children advantages that we didn't have. I promise you that there is nothing in this world that will fill *your* tank with a higher premium fuel than dealing your children a better hand than you received yourself. It's the most fulfilling, positive, loving, enriching and heroic thing you will ever accomplish. You'll feel it every step of the way. Your children will become the best possible versions of themselves, and so will you.

Chapter 9

FOR THE THERAPIST

The concept of Emotional Neglect slowly became visible to me as I practiced psychotherapy over a period of fifteen years. During that time I treated a number of patients who did not seem to benefit enough from the usual tools of our trade: empathy, insight, cognitive therapy, confrontation, family or couples therapy, medication, and so on. These were the clients who I felt unable to fully understand. It seemed there was something essential missing in the clinical picture that would help make sense of the entire person, his symptoms and his pain. It was as if I was the fabled blind man, addressing parts of the elephant, unaware that there was an entire elephant to which I should be attending.

In the end, it was the valiant commitment to treatment on the part of some dedicated clients which helped me to become aware of this underlying issue. These clients were able, despite their counter-dependence, to stay with therapy over a long enough period of time for me to recognize what was occurring under the surface, name it and address it.

As this missing element slowly developed into a full model in my head, I discovered myself thinking of it with the designation Emotional Neglect. I could not recall having read any journal articles or books, or attended any training in which Emotional Neglect had been a focus. Yet it was a term which was familiar and carried a specific meaning for me.

I became curious about whether any science existed to support the observations upon which this model was based. I spent many hours perusing the APA research libraries for journal articles, books, or academic papers that might address Emotional Neglect. The first thing I discovered was that the words *emotion* and *neglect* are often used together in academic and clinical writings, and this helped to explain the sense of familiarity. But rather than the actual phrase "emotional neglect," the two terms typically exist together in this form: emotional abuse and neglect. Looking more carefully into this, it became clear that when emotion is addressed in this area of the literature, it is in the form of an act of commission: emotional abuse. When neglect is addressed, it is of the material and observable variety: physical neglect. I realized that the literature was not addressing the difficult-to-detect, but equally damaging, act of omission: Emotional Neglect.

It was then that I decided to write this book. My intention and hope in writing it was to draw attention to that process mentioned above: omission, the oft-overlooked stepchild of parental error. I was further motivated to share the model by my observation that many of the parents who commit this error of omission are excellent parents in other ways and have the best of intentions, further obfuscating the clinical picture for mental health professionals who are trying to understand their clients.

Over the last ten years, I have become practiced at detecting Emotional Neglect. I have realized that the Emotional Neglect must be treated, but that this is not easy since the patients themselves are focused upon their other, more noticeable symptoms. Many are resistant from the outset to the notion that they were emotionally neglected. Further complicating the treatment is the above-mentioned counter-dependence that is so often a part of Emotional Neglect, as it frequently drives these clients from treatment prematurely.

I have found that when an emotionally neglected client finally recognizes his "elephant" treatment can more easily access his emotional depth. From that point forward, the therapy tends to progress more rapidly. Later in this chapter, I will offer suggestions for how to identify and treat this underlying issue, including how to counter the counter-dependence, and address the shame, guilt and self-blame which tend to go along with Emotional Neglect. But first, let's look at the scientific literature as it relates to this model.

Research

As noted earlier in this chapter, I have been unable to find studies or writings which describe or directly examine the phenomenon of Emotional Neglect. However, Emotional Neglect is closely related to two large areas of the literature. I see its nucleus at the intersection where **attachment theory** and **Emotional Intelligence** meet. Attachment theory offers the best demonstration of how parental acts of omission lead to symptoms of Emotional Neglect. The field of Emotional Intelligence addresses the most pivotal of all of the Emotional Neglect symptoms: lack of emotional awareness and knowledge.

Attachment Theory

The scientific understanding of the human mind has come a long way since John Bowlby wrote *Maternal Care and Mental Health* in 1951. Bowlby's book introduced the notion that an infant's attachment to its mother significantly impacts the personality that the infant will have as an adult. His theory was criticized and questioned by other experts of the day for being based upon too little data. Other scientists were resistant to Bowlby's ideas because they challenged the universally held belief that infants' development was based purely upon their own inner fantasy life, and had nothing to do with external relationships or mothering. Fortunately, a number of other scientists have studied Bowlby's theory since that day. Some have spent many hours and days watching and recording the most subtle interactions between mothers and infants. Using longitudinal methods, they have been able to find some of those exact parent/child subtleties reflected in those same children years later.

Hundreds of studies of the process of attachment have, over the last sixty years, demonstrated the importance of the emotional connection of mothers to their children. In the 1970s, psychiatrist Daniel Stern helped fine-tune our understanding of attachment by using videotaping to identify a process he called "attunement." His definition of attunement involved the mother responding to the infant with emotional expression or behaviors that matched or accurately reflected the baby's emotional state. Stern posited that the mother's emotional attunement, beginning from the point of birth, communicates to the child that he is understood and that his needs will be met. This provides a solid foundation from which the child can spring forward to take risks and explore the world.

Many later researchers, such as Mary Ainsworth (1971) and Isabella and Belsky (1991) have demonstrated the direct connection between parents' attitudes toward emotion and their children's later ability to manage, accept and express their emotions. The plethora of research is such that few, if any, mental health professionals today would question this well-documented truth.

In examining the attachment research, one can find numerous studies examining parents' *out-of-tune* emotional responses, such as inappropriate anger, mismatched emotional assumptions, or inaccurate emotional readings (all parental *actions*). But it is difficult to find research which addresses a parent's *lack* of emotional response, such as not noticing, not responding, or not knowing the child, the types of missing pieces that this book is about. This may be because the absence of something is difficult to observe, much less measure or document. Scientists have understandably found acts of commission more amenable to research than the acts of omission which are so significant in Emotional Neglect.

Given the solid scientific basis and generalized knowledge about attachment amongst professionals in the field, it is surprising how little this valuable concept is understood and utilized by the population at large. To us mental health professionals, it is almost a given that a particular individual's personality issues have roots in her childhood. It would be difficult to find a psychologist, psychiatrist or social worker who has not felt the frustration of trying to lead a client to that understanding, but meeting great resistance.

In my practice I have found that many, if not most clients are very uncomfortable with the notion that their primary caretakers had such a great effect on them. Perhaps acknowledging the incredible power of parents is inherently threatening to us all. If we understand the true impact that our parents had on us, we may feel ourselves alone, disempowered, or even victimized. If we understand the true impact that we have on our own children, we may feel terrified. So, as a people, we lean more toward blaming ourselves for our own issues, and underplaying the impact which we have on our children.

One of my goals for this book is to make attachment theory personal, understandable, and digestible for a greater portion of the population. I believe that many people are held back from healing by their natural resistance to the idea that their childhood still significantly affects them in adulthood. I hope that the emotionally neglected will recognize themselves in the vignettes of the many fine, likable people presented in this book, and see that they too will be made stronger, not weaker, by understanding the true impact that parents have on their children's personalities.

Emotional Intelligence

Daniel Goleman, PhD, in his 1995 book *Emotional Intelligence*, defines Emotional Intelligence as consisting of five skills: knowing one's emotions, managing emotions, motivating oneself, recognizing emotions in others, and handling relationships. An individual who falls short on these skills can be described as having low Emotional Intelligence. As you can see, the concept of low Emotional Intelligence could, then, be considered to be the same as alexithymia as defined in this book.

It is interesting to consider the differences between the Emotional Intelligence concept and the concept of Emotional Neglect. In the writings about Emotional Intelligence (particularly the books written by Goleman), attention is paid to how low Emotional Intelligence develops. The mother/infant interaction described above, via attachment theory, is explored as a direct factor in the development of Emotional Intelligence. Also, Dr. Goleman identifies parental empathy and emotional attunement as factors contributing to Emotional Intelligence, as I do in this book with Emotional Neglect. There is a great deal of overlap, therefore, in the result (Low Emotional Intelligence and Emotional Neglect symptoms) and the cause. Both are brought about by lack of parental empathy and attunement, and both results involve alexithymia.

With the Emotional Neglect concept, I am interested in showing the inner experience of the person who is emotionally neglected as a child, and the psychological impact as it appears in the adult later in life. I am addressing the parental failure of emotional attachment, and observing the developmental etiology from the perspective of clinical psychology. While Goleman considers the effects of the parental emotional failure from the perspective of *emotional knowledge*, I am attending to the resulting constellation of *psychological symptoms*: emptiness, poor self-awareness, lack of self-care, self-directed anger, self-blame, and so on.

People may discover that they have low Emotional Intelligence through workplace training or a boss's evaluation, and they may have the opportunity to learn and develop Emotional Intelligence skills through that same venue. But I believe there are vast numbers of people in the world who have no idea what they're missing or why they don't have it. Ironically, they would *need to have emotional awareness to realize that they don't have emotional awareness.* These are the people I am targeting in this book.

In the writings on Emotional Intelligence, Daniel Goleman and others make a strong case for considering the significance of emotional skills to life success. My goal is different. I am looking to help people who are unknowingly living their lives without those skills, to see the constellation of challenges they've been set up with, stop blaming themselves, and heal themselves and their children.

Identification of Emotional Neglect

As noted previously, it can be difficult to detect Emotional Neglect, particularly as it is often buried beneath depression, anxiety, trauma, marital issues, parenting problems, grief, or some other condition which is not only clearly visible, but also the focus of the client.

The Emotional Neglect Questionnaire at the beginning of this book is designed to assist you in identifying the patients for whom Emotional Neglect is a factor. Please feel free to copy it and use it in your practice. I fully recognize and acknowledge that as of the release of this book, no work has been done to investigate the psychometric validity or reliability of the questionnaire. Nonetheless, I decided to include it in this book because I have found it to be useful in identifying Emotional Neglect in my practice. Use it with full understanding of its psychometric limitations. I have found that a client who scores 6 or above is a good candidate for some level of Emotional Neglect, warranting further exploration.

In Chapter 3, *The Neglected Child, All Grown Up*, ten signs and symptoms of Emotional Neglect were discussed. Some of these signs are less likely to be reported or even perceived by the clients themselves. These are signs which are far more likely to be spotted by the therapist. Here are some hallmarks to watch for in your work with your patients.

1. Expressing guilt, discomfort or self-directed anger for having feelings

Many emotionally neglected clients have apologized for crying in front of me during their therapy sessions. It is not unusual for them to precede statements of emotion with an apology, such as, "I feel terrible to say this, but I didn't really want to go to the family reunion"; "I know this is wrong, but I felt like walking out"; "I know this means I'm a bad person, but I get really angry when she does that."

2. Fiercely defending parents from therapist interpretations

The emotionally neglected are desperate to protect their parents from blame. Since they don't remember what their parents *didn't do*, they tend to view their parents as somewhat ideal, and are naturally driven to blame themselves for their struggles. When therapy gets close to identifying ways in which his parents may have failed him, the emotionally neglected client is quick to explain that his parents "did the best they could" or "aren't to blame." This is his way of preserving his deeply held belief that *he* is to blame for whatever he feels is wrong with him.

3. Doubting the substance of their memories from childhood

In my experience, many emotionally neglected patients have difficulty recalling specific things about their childhoods. Often they will report that their childhood feels like a blur that's hard to differentiate into exact events. Furthermore, the emotionally neglected often distrust their own emotional read on the childhood memories that they do have. When they're reporting their mother's temper, their father's workaholism, etc., they often pause to question the reality, importance or validity of their memory. "I feel like I'm probably exaggerating it. It wasn't really that bad," one woman said to me while tears were rolling down her cheeks. "Isn't this boring for you to listen to?" one man said to me while telling me about his parents' lack of reaction to the death of his dog when he was ten. Or, "I don't know why I'm telling you this, it's probably not important," another man said while relaying a story about how his cherished stepfather disappeared from his life after divorcing his mother.

4. Lacking understanding of how emotions work; their own as well as others'

As discussed above, the emotionally neglected are apt to have a low Emotional Intelligence quotient. But it is very difficult for the emotionally neglected to realize that their emotional understanding is poor. They grew up in families in which this was the case, and they've lived their lives this way. So it is vital for therapists to identify alexithymia for patients with Emotional Neglect and to name it for them. Here are some signs:

- repeated physical discomfort (may be evidenced by squirming or fidgeting) when experiencing an emotion in your office
- telling emotionally intense stories in a way that is completely devoid of emotional content
- changing the subject quickly or resorting to humor when the therapist steers the discussion in an emotional direction
- Showing a repeated inability to give answers to feeling-oriented questions. This may consist of giving intellectualized or avoidant answers

  Example: Intellectualized Response
  Q: "What did you feel when she told you to leave?"
  A: "I thought she was being a jerk"
  Example: Avoidant Response
  Q: "What did you feel when she told you to leave?"
  A: "I hadn't realized she was that angry until she said that"

5. Counter-dependence

In my experience the emotionally neglected, more than any other clients, feel upset with themselves for needing my help. Their counter-dependence asserts itself into the treatment relationship, and I have found that to be both unfortunate and fortunate. The unfortunate part is that it can be difficult to keep the emotionally neglected in treatment; the fortunate part is that I have been able to use my relationship with them to directly challenge, and help them work through, their shame and counter-dependence.

The emotionally neglected client may see her need for therapy as weak, pathetic, shameful, foolish or frivolous. Listen for, "Shouldn't I be over this by now?" or, "I'll bet not many thirty-seven-year-olds are still trying to learn how to say no," or my favorite, "I don't like feeling that I *need* you. I want to stop treatment for a while, to make sure I can do it on my own." In my experience, it can be difficult sometimes to keep them coming despite the fact that I, and even they, can see that therapy is helping them. There will be suggestions for how to use the counter-dependence in the treatment in the next section.

6. Memories

As with other diagnoses and conditions, identifying Emotional Neglect from clients' memories can be difficult. This is especially true since when you ask clients about their childhood, they will naturally tend to relate *events* from that time period. As you know, it can be difficult to glean what didn't happen from their stories about what happened. But here are some suggestions for indications to listen for within their memories:

- Memories of a parent drastically misunderstanding the child's feelings, needs or personality. One young woman about to obtain her bachelors degree in social work told me about her parents' pressure upon her all through middle and high school to skip college and take over her father's brick delivery service. I found myself wondering whether these parents had any idea at all who their daughter was.

- Memories that entail the parent negating, ignoring or over-simplifying the child's emotions. For example, one neglectful mother said to her son, "Your big sister misses her father" soon after their father suddenly passed away, paying no heed whatsoever to the feelings of her son.

- Memories of a parent having a favorite phrase that squelches the child's emotional expression, like "don't be a baby" or "get over it" or "stop crying". (Note that many mindful parents might use these phrases on occasion; it must be either used extremely inappropriately just once, or used frequently, to indicate that it represents a general philosophy of Emotional Neglect.)

- Memories that convey significant feelings of deprivation in some non-physical area that was important to the patient as a child. "I was fascinated with the guitar but my mom insisted that I be a violin player," for example, or "I *really* wanted to be with my friends in middle school but my parents were very strict."

- Memories that seem unimportant but have a lot of emotion attached to them. Kathleen in Chapter 1 relayed a memory about sandplay with her dad at the beach. On the surface it seemed trivial, but it was the lack of emotional attunement from her parents that made it memorable for her. Watch for these types of intense but seemingly meaningless memories, because they are often remembered by the patient specifically because they are loaded with the invisible pain of Emotional Neglect.

With increasing frequency, I find my clients entering treatment having already diagnosed themselves. Some people are able to see on their own that they are depressed or have anxiety. But it is unusual for a client to identify Emotional Neglect for himself. It is my hope that therapists will stay alert to the possibility of Emotional Neglect in their clients, and that the above suggestions will be helpful in identifying it.

Treatment

1. Treat the Presenting Problem First

In most cases, the therapist will see the Emotional Neglect before the patient does. Since it is difficult for many clients to see their own Emotional Neglect even after it's been pointed out by the therapist, it can be problematic to try to make it a focus early in the therapy. I have found that the concept of Emotional Neglect is, like other painful insights, best accepted by the client after a strong therapeutic alliance has been developed. While treating the presenting problem, the therapist will have the opportunity to point out examples of Emotional Neglect as they arise. Piece by piece, the case will be built so that when the full concept of Emotional Neglect is finally presented to the client, it can become a meaningful, useful model for understanding himself.

2. Counter the Counter-dependence

Because of the counter-dependence, it is a general tendency for emotionally neglected clients to leave treatment as soon as they feel some relief from their presenting problem. I believe that the best way to treat counter-dependence is to work hard to keep emotionally neglected patients in therapy as long as they are benefitting, while continuously pointing out and challenging their counter-dependence every step of the way.

Therapists may sometimes find that it requires a significant amount of energy to simply keep emotionally neglected clients from terminating treatment before they are ready. But for the emotionally neglected, keeping them in therapy not only allows them to *do* the work of therapy, it *is* the work of therapy. In essence, the Emotional Neglect patient will benefit greatly from experiencing a healthy dependence on her therapist which, as a child, she was not able to *feel* with her parents.

Each time the patient makes one of the counter-dependent statements listed above (in the section on counter-dependence) in the therapy, it's very important to catch it and address it directly. She may make this comment in many different ways, at different points in the treatment. Each time she says it, she is offering the therapist an opportunity to address one of her core issues (counter-dependence) from a different angle. Here are questions that have helped me access this core issue:

Do you think it's bad to need another person's help? Why?

Where in your childhood did you get the message that you shouldn't need help?

What does needing me, relying on me, depending on me make you feel?

Were there any people in your childhood upon whom you felt comfortable relying?

Do you think everyone else has already worked out all their issues?

Would you judge your friend for going to therapy?

Do you believe there's a time limit for therapy?

Do you know what counter-dependence is? (Then name it and define it for her.)

Are you afraid that I'll disappoint you? Abandon you? Hurt you in some way?

Are you worried that I might be judging you for needing help?

Why do you hold yourself to impossible standards?

Do you realize that you're not allowing yourself to be human?

These are some examples, but there are an infinite number of ways to challenge the counter-dependence. Of course the client will make the decision in the end. But the point is that the therapist will need to take every opportunity to address counter-dependence head-on. I have found that it is most helpful to think of my patients' difficulty staying in therapy not as an inconvenience, but as an opportunity.

3. Build Tolerance for Emotion

Cognitive-behavioral, psychodynamic, psychoanalytic, medical, substance abuse, family, marriage, inpatient, outpatient or day-treatment mental health professionals all deal with a lot of emotion in their practices. While it is true that most people come to therapy for reasons involving difficulties with emotional health, the emotionally neglected patient can be particularly challenging in the specific area of emotional knowledge and tolerance. Since the language of emotion is so foreign and the experience of emotion is so uncomfortable, this aspect of treatment can be the most challenging.

I suggest a gradual exposure model when it comes to helping the emotionally neglected client become more comfortable with feelings. In terms of therapeutic style, think of this as systematic desensitization, as opposed to implosive therapy. I have used the Identifying & Naming Exercise (Chapter 6, Section 3) with a number of emotionally neglected clients in my office. Conducting this exercise during a session can be useful in two ways: assessing the client's ability to sit with and report emotion, and building tolerance for emotion. One emotionally neglected client, when asked to sit with me, close his eyes, focus inward and ask himself what he was feeling, immediately opened his eyes wide and said, "I just went totally numb." It was a lightbulb moment in the treatment, for both him and me. At that moment we knew our starting point, and we continued to use this exercise throughout the treatment, with the initial goal of not going numb.

It is very important for the therapist to point out emotion when you see or hear it in a session. Many therapists do this regularly, and with the emotionally neglected client, it is of special importance. Speak the language of emotion in the therapy. Ask the client what he thinks someone else was feeling. Ask him what he himself was feeling. Ask him what he *is* feeling, right here, right now. (The previous three questions are placed in order of least to most difficult for the emotionally neglected patient.)

I have found that it is very helpful to ask these clients what they were feeling when certain events happened in their childhood. For example, remember Kathleen with the sandplay memory from Chapter 1, who was able to identify the reasons for her adult anger at her mother by being asked in therapy to describe her emotional response to a seemingly innocuous statement her mother made in childhood. Or Simon from Chapter 3, who was irritated by my emotion-based questions in therapy, but who was finally, in the end, healed by those very questions. Reflect your client's feelings back to her when she is unaware. "You're saying it's no big deal, yet you look really sad about it," or "You say it didn't bother you, yet I can hear the anger in your voice." Additionally it is very important for the therapist to allow himself to feel while he is with the client, and to be authentic with his own emotional responses (while keeping the therapeutic boundary, of course.)

4. Provide Mirroring

This aspect of the treatment ties together several previously discussed facets of Emotional Neglect, all of which involve increasing self-knowledge. This is not the same issue or process as identity. I have found that emotionally neglected patients typically have a well-developed identity; the problem is that they are not familiar enough with it.

As discussed previously, the emotionally neglected adult typically grew up without accurate feedback from his primary caregivers regarding who he is. This leaves him with either distorted self-knowledge or very little self-knowledge. As adults in treatment, they may struggle to define what they want, what they can and can't do, and who they actually are.

In this regard, it can be useful to talk about the parental mirror with the emotionally neglected client directly. Since it is hard for the client to see what *wasn't* reflected back, the concept of the parental mirror can provide her with a clear, visual sense of what didn't happen for her. Once the client understands what she didn't get, the therapist can help her complete her own picture by becoming the mirror for her.

This means carefully observing everything about, for example, her preferences, learning style, cognitive style, aesthetics, strengths, weaknesses, and relational style. Then feed it back to her whenever possible, in a manner that she can take in. She may see herself reflected in the therapist's eyes, or learn about herself via the therapist's verbal observations. Either way, she will gradually become more familiar with who she is.

Along with this, it's important to make sure that the client knows that *in total, in the big picture* she has quality. She must get the message from her therapist that it's okay if she has weaknesses and faults and if she dislikes some things or people. She still has other strengths and other things and people that she does like. This is the sense of balanced self-view and self-esteem that will sustain her through challenges, disappointments, and even failures.

5. Provide the Balanced Healthy Parental Voice

One of the most vital things missing from the internal world of the emotionally neglected adult is the balanced, integrated inner voice that we are all meant to have, which talks us through difficult times, helps us understand and learn from our mistakes, and in some ways serves as our own personal sounding board. Living life without this emotional anchor can leave the emotionally neglected untethered and vulnerable to life's challenges. Many emotionally neglected clients have expressed to me a feeling that they are not in control of their own lives, that they go where the tide takes them, and simply try to make the best of wherever they end up. Remember Josh in Chapter 3, who had great difficulty choosing and committing to a career, and then stopped teaching as soon as he received some criticism? Or Noelle, also in Chapter 3, who became paralyzed by her own harsh internal voice? Neither Josh nor Noelle had a parent who reflected back, talked them through their mistakes, or gave them a balanced, reality-based voice which they could internalize. As adults, they each had difficulty staying resilient through life's challenges.

An important part of the treatment of the emotionally neglected is therefore providing them with that balanced voice. The therapist should lead the client through an examination of his negative experience, whether it is a criticism, failure or mistake. Help him consider the reasons the event occurred, and what to do about it, while maintaining an integrated, compassionate stance. Each time this happens, the client will have the opportunity to learn how to think through these types of situations for himself in a balanced, thoughtful, compassionate manner. This will help him become less likely to make the same mistake, or to fold when faced with a challenge in the future.

6. Resist the Urge to Indulge Your Client

Why I am suggesting that the therapist might have such an urge? The answer has nothing to do with the therapist; it has everything to do with the emotionally neglected client. As we've talked about before, emotionally neglected clients tend to go back and forth between extreme self-castigation and letting themselves completely off the hook. As therapists, our goal is to neutralize both of those internal voices by providing a third alternative voice, a voice which holds the client accountable in a balanced and caring way, a voice which compassionately speaks the truth.

The emotionally neglected client, as evidenced by the above back and forth process, not only has a ruthless internal voice; she also is skilled at self-indulgence. She will have an unconscious tendency to pull for the therapist to not hold her accountable. In her mind she has two choices: she is either absolved or excoriated. It is understandable that she would repeatedly choose to be absolved of any wrongdoing. Furthermore, since the emotionally neglected client is probably quite likable, the therapist might find it difficult to hold her accountable. But if the therapist notices that she is not trying her hardest, for example, he must say, "I believe you can do better." When the therapist sees her making poor choices, he must speak the truth for her and help her think it through. When the therapist sees her being too easy on herself, he must tell her this in a caring way, in a way that neutralizes the two extreme sides of her own internal voice and creates a third voice, compassionate, yet firm and challenging.

7. Challenge Self-Castigation
This natural aspect of most therapy becomes particularly important with the emotionally neglected. The therapist must stay vigilant to every word, every implication, every facial expression and every subtle overtone which signals that the patient may be beating himself up, by either word or thought. When this occurs with the therapist present, it is an opportunity for the therapist to make the patient aware of the self-destructive voice and the damage it is doing. After building the client's awareness, it will be more effective when the therapist models the words, balance and strength to be found in self-compassion. The goal is for him to internalize this voice so that over time it will become his own.

Summary for the Therapist

- Watch for the subtle signs.
- If you suspect Emotional Neglect, use the diagnostic tool
- Point out the signs of Emotional Neglect with care while you treat the presenting condition.
- Be the mirror to build self-knowledge.
- Be the voice of balance, compassion and challenge.
- Don't indulge, but continually challenge self-blame and self-directed anger.
- Counter the counter-dependence.
- Welcome, speak and build tolerance for emotion.
- Provide the watchful, caring, reality-based relationship that he did not have with his parents.
- Help him build self-compassion and self-care.

Conclusion

I hope that my concept of Emotional Neglect will resonate with the experience of other clinicians, and that it will spark the curiosity of researchers. There are several testable assumptions underlying this model:

- What is the frequency with which the identified Emotional Neglect symptoms occur together?
- Is that frequency at a high enough level to suggest that they are related to each other via an underlying syndrome?
- What is the correlation between the results of the Emotional Neglect Questionnaire and therapists' independent perception of Emotional Neglect in their clients?
- Does the Emotional Neglect Questionnaire have inter-rater reliability and validity?
- Can the Emotional Neglect Questionnaire's reliability and validity be improved by adding or subtracting certain questions?
- Does treatment progress better when the concept of Emotional Neglect is utilized appropriately by the therapist?

These are just a few of the questions that I believe warrant scientific examination. I am highly interested in pursuing them, and hope that others will be similarly motivated.

My greatest hope for this book is that it will advance the concept of Emotional Neglect, bringing it out of the darkness and into the light. And, most importantly, that it will bring clarity, self-awareness, solace and strength to many well-deserving people who have not yet realized what they never got in childhood.

RESOURCES
FOR RECOVERY

For more about Emotional Neglect and recovery:
www.drjonicewebb.com

Assertiveness book:
Alberti, Robert E. Your Perfect Right: Assertiveness and Equality in Your Life and Relationships (9th Edition). California: Impact Publishing, 2008.

Relationship improvement book:
Real, Terrence. The New Rules of Marriage: What You Need to Know to Make Love Work. New York: Ballantine Books, 2008.

Feeling Word List:

SAD	Desperate	Grave	Grey
Tearful	Low	Dismayed	Miserable
Sorrowful	Pessimistic	Bummed	Blue
Pained	Unhappy	Despondent	Longing
Grief	Grieved	Heavy-hearted	Disappointed
Anguish	Mournful	Scorned	Grim

Gloomy
Lost
Moody
Burdened
Discouraged
Let down

DEPRESSED
Lousy
Dysphoric
Dreary
Dark
Black
Morose
Dour
Besieged
Morbid
Suicidal
Accursed
Abysmal
Ashamed
Diminished
Self-destructive
Self-abasing
Guilty
Dissatisfied
Loathsome
Worn out
Repugnant
Despicable
Abominable

Terrible
Despairing
Sulky
Bad
Sense of loss

DAMAGED
Aberrant
Maimed
Detestable
Ruined
Defiled
Scarred
Impure
Spoiled
Infected
Scathed
Beleaguered
Impaired
Disgusting
Crippled
Abhorred
Destroyed
Abnormal
Contaminated
Contemptible

UNCOM-FORTABLE
Awkward
Discomfit

Antsy
Disturbed
Sickened
Off-balance
Sour
Fidgety
Peculiar
Icky
Ill-tempered
Odd
Inappropriate
Out of it
Conspicuous
Off-center
Rotten
Discontented

ANGRY
Misanthropic
Miffed
Irritated
Contemptuous
Fiery
Spiteful
Perturbed
Abrasive
Stewing
Seething
Livid
Confrontive
Pissed off

Bristling
Dangerous
Galled
Bugged
Disgruntled
Contentious
Abusive
Enraged
Surly
Bloodthirsty
Hostile
Insulting
Disgusted
Exasperated
Repulsed
Steamed
Dismayed
Frustrated
Revolted
Troubled
Cranky
Horrified
Furious
Outraged
Ticked off
Riled
Nauseated
Vicious
Wary
Sore
Annoyed

Upset
Hateful
Unpleasant
Offensive
Bitter
Aggressive
Aggravated
Appalled
Resentful
Inflamed
Provoked
Incensed
Infuriated
Cross
Worked up
Boiling
Fuming

BORED
Mundane
Listless
Under-
stimulated
Dreary
Tedious
Unchallenged
Bland

HURTFUL
Mean
Enraged

Rude
Retaliatory
Menacing
Ruthless
Mouthy
Nasty
Dangerous
Vengeful
Offensive
Malicious
Malignant
Malevolent
Cruel
Manipulative
Sadistic
Harmful
Controlling

VULNERABLE
Exposed
Bullied
Corralled
Small
Susceptible
Expendable
Bare
Raw
Delicate
One-upped
Weak
Obscured

Little
Eclipsed
Controlled
Conned
Conspicuous
Sensitive
Constrained
Blind
Bested
Lost
Broken
One-down
Open
Captive

**EMBAR-
RASSED**
Humiliated
Ashamed
Clumsy
Uncomfortable
Mortified
Awkward
Silly
Disgraced
Conspicuous
Foolish
Absurd

GUILTY
Undeserving

Responsible
Rueful
Contrite
Regretful
Accountable
Remorseful
Culpable
Deceitful
Wrong
At fault
Faulty

ALONE
Abandoned
Antisocial
Outnumbered
Loveless
Estranged
Bypassed
Dissociated
Longing
Inaccessible
Friendless
Needy
Disregarded
Distant
Alienated
Desolate
Avoided
Apart
Disliked

Deserted
Aloof
Ignored
Dispossessed
Rejected
Isolated
Excluded
Jilted

LOST
Rudderless
Planless
Scattered
Seeking
Stranded
Stumped

CONFUSED
Ambivalent
Puzzled
Uncertain
Conflicted
Indecisive
Hesitant
Misgiving
Lost
Unsure
Uneasy
At a loss
Tense
Perplexed

Flustered
Confused
Befuddled
Disconcerted
Mystified
Bewildered
Anxious
Muddled
Baffled
Addled
Distracted
Doubtful

SHOCKED
Agape
Aghast
Agog
Flabbergasted
Stricken
Jolted
Stunned
Dumbstruck
Startled
Jarred
Astonished
Rattled
Dumbfounded
Dazed
Stupefied
Dumfounded
Astounded

Awestruck

NEGATIVE
Averse
Hesitant
Against
Opposed
Quarrelsome
Resistant
Disharmonious
Rebellious
Oppositional
Stubborn
Recalcitrant

TIRED
Battle-worn
Worn
Overdrawn
Drained
Stretched
Pooped
Strained
Faint
Bedraggled
Dried up
Listless
Limp
Overloaded
Harried
Hassled

Downtrodden
Depleted
Exhausted
Done-in
Fried
Weary
Finished
Dispirited
Spent
Careworn
Used up

AFRAID
Fear
Boxed-in
Cornered
Chilled
Suspicious
Anxious
Doubtful
Cowardly
Quaking
Menaced
Wary
Frightened
Jittery
Jumpy
Scared
Threatened
Terrified
Spooked

Shaken

Uneasy

Overwhelmed

Alarmed

Worried

ANXIOUS

Daunted

Timid

Knotted

Self-conscious

Neurotic

Restless

Fretful

Stressed

Guarded

Ruffled

Skittish

Preoccupied

Frantic

Pell-mell

Obsessive

Shy

Overcome

Shaky

Jangled

Insecure

Nervous

Dreading

Panicky

Unnerved

Cautious

Antsy

HURT

Invalidated

Chastised

Invisible

Ridiculed

Screwed

Wronged

Abased

Punched

Humiliated

Squashed

Burned

Blamed

Annihilated

Rebuffed

Brutalized

Bushwhacked

Laughed at

Agonized

Heart-broken

Disrespected

Victimized

Insulted

Jilted

Cheated

Devalued

Forgotten

Intimidated

Neglected

Defeated

Persecuted

Put down

Oppressed

Slighted

Aching

Afflicted

Injured

Offended

Rejected

Assaulted

Dejected

Tortured

Pained

Deprived

Tormented

Bleeding

Crushed

Abused

Damaged

Ignored

Snubbed

Diminished

Betrayed

Deflated

VICTIMIZED

Bullied

Quashed

Mistreated

Scapegoated

Eviscerated

Jinxed

Hoodwinked

Suffocated

Intruded upon

Erased

Set up

Objectified

Railroaded

Reamed

Denounced

Emasculated

Controlled

Denigrated

Deceived

Bamboozled

Abused

Crushed

Duped

Devoured

Dumped-on

Cuckolded

Cursed

Degraded

Damned

Debased

Cheated

Cheated on

Deprived

Crucified

INADEQUATE
Mediocre
Unworthy
Incompetent
Spineless
Insecure
Meek
Insufficient
Powerless
Helpless
Inferior
Incapable
Useless
Inept
Unworthy
Weak
Pathetic
Worthless
One-down
Deficient
Enfeebled
Second rate

HELPLESS
Incapable
Controlled
Stifled
Impotent
Paralyzed
Straight-
jacketed

Stuck
Stonewalled
Micro-managed
Lame
Useless
Vulnerable
Hindered
Immobile
Ineffective
Futile
Forced
Despairing
Distressed
Pathetic
Dominated
Tragic
Woeful
Frustrated
Hesitant
Empty
Inferior
Fatigued
Alone
Overwhelmed

INDIFFERENT
Apathetic
Lifeless
Empty
Bland
Robotic

Dead
Disinterested
Emotionless
Lackadaisical
Banal
Blasé
Cavalier
Cold
Bored
Absent
Neutral
Weary
Reserved
Nonchalant
Insensitive
Uncaring
Dulled
Mindless

HAPPY
Joyous
Mirthful
Peachy
Fortunate
Giddy
Exuberant
Buoyant
Delighted
Overjoyed
Gleeful
Thankful

Festive
Ecstatic
Satisfied
Glad
Cheerful
Sunny
Merry
Perky
Jubilant
Elated
Delirious
Soaring
Important
Lucky
Great
Sparkling
Bouncy
Blissful

OPEN
Understanding
Ready
Confident
Reliable
Kind
Accepting
Receptive
Satisfied
Sympathetic
Adventurous
Fun-loving

Boundless
Exultant
Interested
Free
Amazed
Easy
Aboard

ALIVE
Playful
Courageous
Energetic
Glowing
Spunky
Liberated
Optimistic
Peppy
Reborn
Provocative
Impulsive
Free
Frisky
Animated
Electric
Spirited
Thrilled
Wonderful
Awake
Colorful
Glorious

GOOD
Serene
Relaxed
Deserving
Calm
Decent
Pleasant
At ease
Comfortable
Pleased
Clean
Fabulous
Encouraged
Surprised
Extraordinary
Smart
Clever
Content
Quiet
Bright
Pleased
Reassured
Sure
Certain

LOVING
Considerate
Admiration
Passionate
Devoted
Attracted

Cuddly
Tender
Sensitive
Caring
Affectionate
Love
Connection
Warmth

INTERESTED
Engrossed
Snoopy
Nosy
Concerned
Affected
Intrigued
Fascinated
Inquisitive
Rapt
Absorbed
Curious
Attentive
Aware
Imaginative

STRONG
Hardy
Tenacious
Resolute
Stable
Authoritative

Persevering
Revitalized
Brave
Unique
Dynamic
Nervy
Moral
Influential
Feisty
Rebellious
Outspoken
Sure
Ethical
Certain
Free
Clear
Graceful
In control
Confrontive
Reliable
Able
Accomplished
Assertive
Assured
Solid
Capable
Competent
Courageous
Hardy

POSITIVE
Enthusiastic
Excited
Eager
Keen
Earnest
Intent
Anxious
Determined
Inspired
Complimented
Productive
Pumped
Sincere
Hopeful

ACCEPTABLE
Adequate
Okay
Good enough
Average
Functional
Legitimate

CARED FOR
Admired
Pampered
Appreciated
Accom-
modated
Esteemed

Honored

THANKFUL
Appreciative
Grateful
Obliged
Beholden
Owing

SMART
Heady
Intelligent
Bright
Accurate
Brainy
Focused
Brilliant
Knowing
Decisive
Clear
Quick
Informed
Observant
Articulate
Imaginative
Logical
Mature
Sagacious
Wise
Skilled
Thoughtful

Sensible

CARING
Benevolent
Loving
In tune
Connected
Empathetic
Selfless
Sympathetic
Gracious
Dedicated
Attached
Loyal
Generous
Affectionate
Responsible
Warm
Nurturing
Cuddly
Communi-
cative

RELAXED
Calm
Breezy
Sleepy
Released
Chill
Resolved

ATTRACTIVE
Captivating
Pretty
Funny
Jazzy
Irresistible
Handsome
Good-looking
Desirable
Appealing
Popular
Lovely
Beautiful
Hot
Gorgeous
Interesting
Dandy
Sexy
Dapper
Well-dressed
Coordinated
Stylish
Debonair

REFERENCES

Ainsworth, Mary. "Infant-Mother Attachment and Social Development: Socialization as a Product of Reciprocal Responsiveness to Signals." *The Integration of a Child into a Social World.* London: Cambridge University Press, 1974.

Baumrind, Diana. "Effects of Authoritative Parental Control on Child Behavior." *Child Development* 37.4 (1966): 887-907.

Bowlby, John. *Maternal Care and Mental Health.* Northvale, NJ: J. Aronson, 1995.

Goleman, Daniel. *Emotional Intelligence.* New York: Bantam, 2005.

Isabella, Russell and Jay Belsky. "Interactional Synchrony and the Origins of Infant-Mother Attachments: A Replication Study." *Child Development* 62 (1991): 373-394.

Jacques, Sharon. *Horizontal and Vertical Questioning.* Couples Treatment Seminar, 2002.

Linden, David J. *The Compass of Pleasure: How Our brains Make Fatty Foods, Orgasm, Exercise, Marijuana, Generosity, Vodka, Learning, and Gambling Feel so Good.* New York: Viking, 2011.

McKay, Matthew and Patrick Fanning. *Self-esteem.* Oakland, CA: New Harbinger Publications, 1993.

National Institute of Health. National Institute of Mental Health. *Suicide in the U.S. Statistics and Prevention.* Bethesda, MD: National Institute of Mental Health, 2007.

Pleis, JR, Ward, BW and Lucas, JW. "Summary health statistics for U.S. adults: National Health Interview Survey, 2009." National Center for Health Statistics. Vital Health Stat 10(249). 2010.

Stern, Daniel N. *The Interpersonal World of the Infant: A View from Psychoanalysis and Development Psychology.* New York: Basic, 2000.

Stout, Martha. *The Sociopath Next Door.* New York: Broadway, 2006.

Taylor, Jill Bolte. *My Stroke of Insight: A Brain Scientist's Personal Journey.* New York: Viking, 2008.

Thoreau, Henry David. *Walden.* Ticknor and Fields: Boston, 1854.

Winnicott, D.W. *The Child, the Family, and the Outside World.* New York: Perseus Group, 1992.

Free Excerpt of Dr. Jonice Webb's New Book,
RUNNING ON EMPTY NO MORE

Healing your Childhood Emotional Neglect has a way of changing almost everything in your life for the better. Learning to accept your emotions paves the way to improving your marriage, your parenting, and maybe even your relationship with your own parents.

That's why I wrote my second book, ***Running On Empty No More: Transform Your Relationships.*** Below is the Introduction to the book.

Introduction to
Running On Empty No More: Transform Your Relationships

In 2012 I wrote *Running on Empty: Overcome Your Childhood Emotional Neglect.* Since the day of its publication, I have received thousands of messages from readers who are relieved to finally understand what's been weighing on them for their entire lives.

Some of these folks have had epiphanies that turned their lives around by dramatically alleviating their shame and confusion, and setting them on a forward path. For others it's been more of a series of quiet realizations taking them out of the darkness and into the light of self-understanding and strength.

Beginning to feel your emotions is no small thing. In fact, it's deceptively tremendous. As you chip away the wall that your child self built to block out your emotions, you begin to feel more and more valid, and more and more alive.

If you started out feeling little to nothing, you can find yourself a bit disconcerted by these new experiences. Bit by bit, you find yourself feeling the weight of sadness in your chest, the zing of excitement in your belly, or perhaps some anger or hurt from past wrongs that were done you. Some of these emotions can be painful, yes. Others are joyous and loving. All of them, positive and negative, connect you to your true self, to the world, and to the people around you in a new way that you never imagined.

Everyone is different, of course. But one factor is shared by all who are on the path of CEN Recovery: all are changing their lives by changing themselves on the inside. And changing on the inside has ripple effects on the outside. Every positive, healthy change that you make in yourself affects the people around you. This can lead to some very unexpected challenges.

And that is the reason for this book.

Before we go on, a quick refresher on Childhood Emotional Neglect (or CEN). CEN is as simple in its definition as it is devastating in its effects.

Childhood Emotional Neglect is what happens when, throughout your childhood, your parents fail to respond *enough* to your emotional needs.

What happens to you as a child, growing up in a household that is either blind to your emotions or intolerant of what you feel? You must adapt to your situation. To ensure that you don't burden your parents with your feelings or emotional needs, you push your emotions down and away. You become intolerant of your own feelings, and you try hard to have no needs.

Most likely all of this happens outside of your conscious awareness. Your little child brain knows exactly what to do to protect you, and how to do it. A metaphorical wall is constructed to block your feelings away, protecting your parents from needing to deal with them. This automatic, adaptive move may serve you quite well in your childhood home, but as an adult, you will suffer.

Living life with your own feelings partially walled off is painful and challenging. Your emotions, which should be connecting you, motivating you, stimulating and guiding you, are not available enough to do their job. You find yourself living in a world that seems less bright, less vivid, and less interesting than the world you see others enjoying. You struggle to know what you want, what you need, or how to thrive. Indeed, you find yourself running on empty.

These natural effects of having your emotions walled off can also be quite baffling. Especially if your parents provided for you well materially, or if they loved you and did their best while raising you, you will struggle to understand why you're not happier, and why you feel different from others in some unnamable way. "What am I missing that others seem to have? What is wrong with me?"

The reality is that what you are missing is the most vital thing you need in order to have rewarding, resilient, meaningful relationships. You are missing ready access to your emotions. A CEN relationship can often be described as a watered-down version of what a relationship should be. Sadly, most CEN couples don't realize this, since it's all they have ever known.

Wondering if you have CEN?

CEN can be invisible and hard to remember, so it can be difficult to know if you have it. If what you have read so far rings true to you, I invite you to visit drjonicewebb.com/cen-questionnaire and take the Emotional Neglect Questionnaire.

To learn how the CEN adaptive pattern in childhood continues to affect you throughout your adult years and how to heal it, see my first book, *Running on Empty: Overcome Your Childhood Emotional Neglect.*

If you've already realized that CEN is a part of your life and are experiencing some of the benefits of addressing it, or if you suspect that someone you care about has CEN, read on. Because this book is for you.

Recovery from CEN is a process. As you recover, you start to feel differently and act differently. As you get in touch with your feelings, you have more energy, more motivation and more direction. As you get to know yourself better, you realize that you have wishes and needs, and what those wishes and needs are. As you realize that you're not weak or damaged after all, you start feeling good about taking up more space. You start to realize that you are just as valid and important as everyone else. You start feeling closer to the people around you, and you may start wanting more emotional substance back from them.

As you're working hard, cleaning up all of the havoc that CEN has wreaked throughout the decades of your life, you can't help but wreak more havoc of a different kind. It's a healthy kind of havoc that's brought on by the healthy changes you are making. Yet it's havoc nonetheless.

The transformation of the CEN person may be dramatic, may be slow and steady, may be intermittent/sporadic, or may be all three at different times. But no matter how you transform your inner self, it affects the people who are closest to you. They may become puzzled, confused or surprised by you. They may sense different feelings, or a different depth of feelings coming from you. They may find you more assertive, and they may even resent you for it.

No matter where you are in your recovery, simply becoming aware of your CEN can throw many parts of your life into question. As you see the effects of CEN, you may feel your own relationships disrupted. You may feel angry or guilty or irritated at your parents or your spouse. You may become aware of what you're *not* getting from these people to whom you are the closest. You may become aware of what you've *not* been giving them.

What do you do when you are becoming healthier and changing for the better, and yet you find your life becoming more complex?

The Three Big Questions I Get Most Often:

1. How do I heal the effects of CEN on my relationship?
2. How do I deal with my parents, now that I realize they emotionally neglected me?
3. How do I deal with the effects of CEN that I now see in my children?

Each of these Three Big Questions encompasses many more:

•   I think my husband has CEN. How do I talk with him about it?

- What about the special case in which both partners in a relationship grew up with CEN?
- Should I talk with my parents about Emotional Neglect? How do I do it?
- I feel guilty about how angry I am at my parents. What should I do?
- I can see how CEN has affected the way I've raised my children. Is it too late to fix it?
- I can see the effects of CEN on my adult children. How can I reach out to talk with them about CEN?
- Is it possible to heal the emotional distance in my relationship?

If any of these questions resonate with you, you are not alone. You are in the same boat with many other CEN people like yourself who are working and striving to better their lives.

You are brave, and you are strong. Otherwise you would not be reading this. You deserve guidance, warmth and care. You deserve the answers and help that you were denied in childhood.

It is for you that I write this book.